Everyone wants to be somebody. It's the hidden addiction of our time. When all that crashes and burns—as it will and as it must—**God Loves Nobodies** is cool water. It is a safe place to land. Here the gritty realities of life in this world and the deep hunger of our culture are exposed and met with fresh Scriptures freshly handled. Open this engaging book knowing that the moment is prepared for us each to know more fully who we are to Christ and in Christ, and who is for us.

—Dr. Mark Paustian, Martin Luther College, New Ulm, MN

The best version of anyone is their identity designed and assigned by God's grace. In **God Loves Nobodies** you will find more meaning, purpose, and significance no matter who you are. Packed with cultural illustrations and biblical evidence, it will engage you to better answer the universal and personal question, "Who am I?"

—Pastor Daron Lindemann, Crosslife Church, Pflugerville, TX

Masterfully illustrated with historical, social, cultural, and personal experiences, **God Loves Nobodies** delivers Scripture's message of God's love and his purpose for me in a down-to-earth, practical, and relatable manner. If you're like me, a real person facing real-life issues as you live out your faith, **God Loves Nobodies** has an important message for you as well. I am thankful for the gift that this book will be to Christ's church.

—Rev. Jonathan Bare, Ed.D. Pastoral Studies Institute, Wisconsin Lutheran Seminary, Mequon, WI

My whole life I've felt like someone who never quite fit in. That's why I'm so thankful for this book. It is filled with good news and some good laughs. Pastor Matt shows from Scripture that God sees nobodies, saves nobodies, and even uses nobodies. If you have ever felt like an outsider, read this book.

—Pastor Ben Sadler, Victory of the Lamb Lutheran Church, Franklin, WI

From the moment I started reading the prologue, I knew this book was the real deal. If you're anything like me, you've found yourself regularly searching for "somebody-ness" in all the wrong places. **God Loves Nobodies** *points us back in the right direction. With an amazing gift for storytelling, Matt uses compelling personal anecdotes, powerful Bible stories, and lots of fun (and often funny) pop-culture references to paint the picture of a Savior who made himself a nobody so we no longer have to be. If you've ever felt like a zero—insignificant, rejected, marginalized, maybe even beyond redemption—this book will bless you in ways you've never imagined.*

—Thad Jahns, Director of Career Development,
Wisconsin Lutheran College, Milwaukee, WI

This book is fast-paced and exciting as the author moves from one story to another all the while connecting God's story to each story, and my story and yours. **God Loves Nobodies: Good News for Somebody Like Me** *is an easy read because we all need grace, and because grace is Good News for Somebody Like Me (and You)!*

—Pastor Bill Limmer, Victory of the Lamb
Lutheran Church, Franklin, WI

God Loves Nobodies *is the book I didn't know I needed (I am an aspiring "somebody," after all). In a style that is both relatable and downright enjoyable, Matt offers a word of conviction and heaps of gospel affirmation. I highly recommend this book for somebodies, nobodies, and everybody in between.*

—Aaron Wakeman, Executive Director, Friends Network

God Loves Nobodies

*Good News
for Somebody Like Me*

Matthew Doebler

NORTHWESTERN PUBLISHING HOUSE
Milwaukee, Wisconsin

For Dale, a nobody in this life,
now a king with Christ

Design and layout: Lynda Williams
Image: iStock

All Scripture quotations, unless otherwise indicated, are taken from the Holy Bible, New International Version®, NIV®. Copyright © 1973, 1978, 1984, 2011 by Biblica, Inc.™ Used by permission of Zondervan. All rights reserved worldwide. www.zondervan.com.

The "NIV" and "New International Version" are trademarks registered in the United States Patent and Trademark Office by Biblica, Inc.™

Northwestern Publishing House
N16W23379 Stone Ridge Dr., Waukesha WI 53188-1108
www.nph.net
© 2022 by Northwestern Publishing House
Published 2022
Printed in the United States of America
ISBN 978-0-8100-3141-8

ISBN 978-0-8100-3142-5 (e-book)

22 23 24 25 26 27 28 29 30 31   10 9 8 7 6 5 4 3 2 1

Acknowledgments

Thank you to a whole host of God's somebodies who inspired me and helped me complete this book.

Jesus— for choosing an Egyptian slave girl to experience your first recorded appearance and shepherds to witness your grand entrance.

Christine— for reminding me every day in some way that I truly am somebody in Christ.

Maddie, Sam, and Caleb— We've been there and back again; so thankful to God that we've trod it together. Next year, NZ!

Oliver Thomas— our brave little knight.

Ash— This is your family now. Bwahahahaha! *evilly strums fingers together*

Opa and Oma— for loving a kid who often felt like a nobody in spite of God's promises and the blessings around him. For introducing me to avocados, chopsticks, and authentic chimichangas.

Nana and Papa— for constant encouragement and prayers!

Dave G— for introducing me to nerdy long before nerdy was cool.

Daron L— I strive to coach like you, my Coach.

Ken K— for being my longtime mentor and one of my dearest friends; enjoy your rest!

Curt L— for weekly reminders of God's amazing work in us and through us.

LUGs— Aaron and Mark, you were sent by God at the critical moment.

Ann T— who ends every e-mail prayer for me with a plea for God's blessing and "legions of angels if necessary."

Steve W— my model for confident prayer.

Marty and Rick— for not giving up on a guy who had given up.

EAT team— What is God up to now?

My students— so eager to learn, so patient with the teacher.

Gretchen and Clay, John and Liz— amazing partners in Christ!

Brian— A great example of the humbly confident Somebody in Christ. I look forward to writing together.

Curt J, Ann J, and NPH— for this amazing opportunity.

Table of Contents

Prologue

Dale was a womanizer; he was a pervert; he was self-serving and cruel. He had committed and gotten away with at least two murders that he confessed to me. He loathed most everything and everyone, including God and the church. Evil churned out of him like the roiling black clouds heralding a Midwestern tornado.

For a while, he lived with his cousin next door to our home. I asked my wife, Christine, and our precious daughter, Madeline, to stay inside if they saw Dale out in the yard. On his worst days, he was one of the most frightening people I had ever met in my life.

But when the pressures of life started squeezing him even harder than normal, he asked to meet with me. At first, all he did was curse and vent, his nearly uncontrollable rage threatening to burst its feeble bonds every moment. I was sure we weren't making any headway or ever would.

Then he asked if we could start meeting for breakfast. We would go to one of those small-town restaurants where the coffee sits on a hot plate for hours in two pots: the brown-rimmed one for "leaded"; the orange-rimmed one for "unleaded." You know the kind of restaurant I am talking about—the kind of place frugal people frequent, seeking heartburn and the reminder why they need to start taking better care of themselves. At our little booth, Dale would chain-smoke and rant and scare off all the senior citizens who were just there for the cheap breakfast, the abundant joe, and the good company. We must have been a sight: one guy clean-cut in his polo and khaki pants, sitting up fairly straight and nervously fiddling with the saltshaker; the other guy with a shaved head, covered in the kinds of tattoos that scream "Back off," cursing every other word, the cigarette on his lips erratically bouncing up and down between the profanities.[1]

I was sitting with a nobody, and I often wondered what I was doing there. Yet this was a nobody who would help transform the way I look at God and the world.

---

[1] To any reader under age 30: Yes, people used to smoke in restaurants.

Part 1

The Somebody Problem

William: A man can change his stars. And I won't spend the rest of my life as nothing.

Roland: [points at hanging corpse] *That is nothing. And nothing is right where glory'll take us.*

—A Knight's Tale

The corpus callosum is a broad band of nerve fibers joining the two hemispheres of the human brain. Because Robert was born without one, the left and right sides of his brain did not communicate properly. According to his doctors, it was a miracle he was alive at all. As a result of this rare condition, he had trouble connecting his thoughts the way humans normally do. Additionally, when Robert was young, his father abandoned him and his mother for another woman. Robert had actually learned to play the piano fairly well, but the day his father left was the last day he ever sat down at the keys.

Robert knew he was different from other people. As a result, he often felt like a nobody. So he would do anything he could to prove that he was normal or uniquely talented, even if it meant a little lying once in a while.

For example, one time he overheard that an intelligent teenage girl at his church was failing her high school sign language course. So Robert told this girl's father that he was a sign language expert and could tutor her. Since Robert seemed honest and kind enough, the father agreed. Robert soon began teaching this girl on a regular basis. Crisis averted.

There was only one problem: Robert didn't know sign language—not a single word. In fact, to this day, I have absolutely no idea how he got past the first lesson without them figuring out that something was amiss. It was like having a swim coach who couldn't swim or a blind tennis instructor.

So Robert's pastor took him out for a milkshake at the local drive-in. As they were sitting in the messy family minivan and sipping their Sonic Classic Shakes, the pastor asked him, "Do you really know sign language, Robert?" Robert replied as confidently as a Harvard professor of quantum physics, "Oh, yes, and I am very good at it too." So the pastor decided to quiz him a bit, dusting off a few old signs from the creaky attic of his memory. He figured Robert would at least know the basics—a lot of people know the sign for "I love you" and some of the letters of the alphabet—so he prepared to start with a few simple signs and then build up to more difficult ones to make his point.

He needn't have planned so far ahead.

"Show me the sign for 'who,'" the pastor requested. Robert thought for a bit. Then he shrugged his shoulders, raised his palms upward in a questioning way, and said, "Who?" like a peppy barn owl. That's right; he didn't know a single word. Of course, anyone who knows even a little bit of sign language knows this is not the sign for *who*—not any more than running around in circles waving your arms back and forth like one of those wacky waving inflatable arm flailing tube men is sign language for "Help! My house is on fire, and my dog is trapped inside!"[2] It only took a single sign, and the pastor had made his point.

As silly as this situation was, it broke the pastor's heart to see such a friendly young man so embarrassed by his wild fantasy of being a respected teacher. He spent the next half hour comforting Robert with some of the truths we will discuss in this book.

But it begs the question: Why would Robert make up such a ridiculous yet audacious lie? Because nobody wants to be a nobody. That's the Somebody Problem we all deal with.

---

[2] By the way, that is the actual name of those inflatable men you see at car dealerships. If you don't believe me, look it up on Wikipedia.

Nobody Wants to Be a Nobody

I always wanted to be somebody, but now I realize I should have been more specific.

—Lily Tomlin

In 2004, the prank collective group known as Improv Everywhere pulled off an elaborate stunt to give one band their 15 minutes of fame. Their target was Ghosts of Pasha, a rock band from Burlington, Vermont. Ghosts of Pasha (GOP) was not what most people would define as a successful group, evidenced by the fact that they were playing a tiny bar at 10 P.M. on a Sunday with an $8 cover charge. No one would be there.

The idea was this: "Pick a struggling rock band and turn their small gig into the best show of their lives."[3] Thirty-five Improv Everywhere members downloaded GOP's EP and memorized the lyrics. Some made T-shirts and temporary tattoos with the band's logo. All 35 showed up as the band was beginning its performance that night; there were only three other paying customers besides them. The pranksters began to sing, dance, request songs, and chant the band's name.

Afterward, guitarist Chris Partyka said, "I don't know about you, but I feel like I have one life to live, and I choose to forever believe in what I felt that night. It's my memory, and just because I was told it wasn't real, doesn't mean it didn't feel real TO ME." For that one night, the band really felt like superstars, like they actually were *somebodies.*

---

[3] https://improveverywhere.com/2004/10/24/best-gig-ever/#1519162039980-e8470d5c-b1c9

Countless people like Chris Partyka are desperate to know they are somebody—to know they are anybody at all. They are desperate that the story of their lives should have meaning, purpose, and significance. It all stems from the question of identity: "Who am I?"—a universal question that haunts people at every age and stage of life, from every culture and background. It's a question that is the topic of regular debate in politics and education, a question that gets near the core of every world religion.

Throughout history, countless stories have been told about a peasant who discovers he is a prince or an ordinary person who becomes a hero. These stories resonate deeply with us because, like Robert, nobody wants to be a nobody. Why do you think that the whole *Star Wars* universe continues to expand with movies, TV shows, and video games? Luke Skywalker is just a poor orphan living on a desert planet with his aunt and uncle. He has big dreams, but in his heart of hearts, he realizes he is a nobody who is going nowhere, until . . . he finds out he has special powers and becomes the key figure in a galactic struggle between good and evil. In the words of the great '80s movie *Can't Buy Me Love,* "He went from totally geek to totally chic."

That trope connected so well with fans that producers decided to try it again, decades later. In 2015, the first movie of the *Star Wars* relaunch, *The Force Awakens,* was virtually the exact same story repackaged—both Luke Skywalker and Rey (the new nobody hero) grow up as orphans on similar desert planets; their wardrobe is practically identical; and both are nearly friendless, aside from the odd, plucky droid. Yet most fans had no complaints at all. We totally identify with this type of story because we want that same narrative for ourselves.

Or think back to the moment of delight when Hagrid tells that neglected orphan living under the stairs, "You're a wizard, Harry!" Only a few pages in, and we're hooked for seven books and eight stretched-out movies. We pick the school houses we want to join (or selected for us by the Sorting Hat): "I'm in Gryffindor!" "I'm in Slytherin!" Many of us pay big money to walk the streets of Diagon Alley and drink sickeningly sweet butterbeer at the Wizarding World of Harry Potter in Florida. Why? Because we want what Harry got; we want to find out that we are somebody.

The hilarious movie *Megamind* is another great example. As their planet is about to be destroyed, a father and mother desperately lay their little baby in an escape pod to save his life. As the world falls to pieces around them, the father proudly tells his boy, "You are destined for . . ." but at that very moment, the hatch of the pod closes, and the confused tyke is unable to hear the rest of his father's proclamation. "I didn't quite hear that last part," he quips, "but it sounded important. Destined for what? I set out to find my destiny." Megamind spends the entire movie on earth trying to discover who he really is. Is he a bad guy? Is he a good guy? What is his purpose? What will his legacy be?

What if, unlike Megamind, you really knew you were somebody—and not just anybody? What if you really knew you were somebody in the eyes of the Greatest Somebody? Wouldn't that be something?

Who are you . . . really?

The life-transforming message of the Bible is that Jesus came to this earth to answer these very questions and solve the Somebody Problem once and for all. The great missionary Paul writes:

> In your relationships with one another, have the same mindset as Christ Jesus: Who, being in very nature God, did not consider equality with God something to be used to his own advantage; rather, he made himself nothing by taking the very nature of a servant, being made in human likeness. And being found in appearance as a man, he humbled himself by becoming obedient to death—even death on a cross! (Philippians 2:5-8)

And "God sent his Son, born of a woman, born under the law, to redeem those under the law, that we might receive adoption to son-ship. So you are no longer a slave, but God's child; and since you are his child, God has made you also an heir" (Galatians 4:4,5,7). The Bible claims that Jesus made himself nothing—a nobody—who was spit on, flogged, and nailed to a wooden cross so that you truly could become somebody—God's very own child along with Jesus.

Fringe is a thriller-style TV show that explores the bizarre world of fringe science. The story arc from episode to episode is often tied together with strange otherworldly men called the Observers. They are agents sent from the far-off future to observe humanity in the present. Because of the danger of tampering with the timeline of the past and negatively impacting their timeline in the future, they are forbidden to interfere in human affairs.[4] However, in one episode, one of the Observers falls in love with a young lady living in our present. After observing her life for years, he begins to see her as a daughter and breaks the Observer ban against developing emotional attachments with their subjects.

Because he is an Observer and can see the future timeline of our universe, he knows that she will soon perish in a horrible plane crash. He cannot stand the thought of losing her. So he kidnaps her to prevent her from going to the airport and boarding that doomed flight. She, her family, the police—everyone, of course—assumes he is a twisted psychopath who intends to harm her in unspeakable ways. The FBI hunts down this apparent madman to apprehend him and free the helpless woman.

Meanwhile, other Observers also hunt down the woman, because she is supposed to die, and tampering with her timeline will most likely affect the future in adverse ways.[5] In the end, the fatherly Observer realizes that the only way his associates won't terminate her is if she is somehow significant to the timeline, if she somehow stands out among the billions of people on our planet. So he sacrifices his life to save her when the assassin arrives to gun her down.

With his final breaths, he asks, "Is she important now?" to which his friend replies, "She must be if you gave your life for her."

---

[4] Nerdy science stuff.

[5] Again, nerdy science stuff. Even more sorry here. I'd like to promise that there are no more nerdy references in this book, but I would be lying.

Jesus' humble life and death definitively answer the question "Am I important?" You must be if God came here and shed his priceless blood for you.

And what was the result of that selfless sacrifice? The missionary Peter writes to those who trust their lives with this Jesus: "You are a chosen people, a royal priesthood, a holy nation, God's special possession, that you may declare the praises of him who called you out of darkness into his wonderful light. Once you were not a people, but now you are the people of God; once you had not received mercy, but now you have received mercy" (1 Peter 2:9,10). Dear Christian, through Jesus, God chose you to be his precious child! He declared you to be royalty, a glorious regent who will inherit heaven and reign forever at Jesus' side. He declared you to be a priest, that is, someone who has direct access to him at any time and has a noble calling to serve as his hands, feet, and voice to the world. God declared you holy—acceptable—to himself through the perfect, proven life of Jesus Christ. He declared you to be his "special possession," his dear friend whom he cherishes every single day of your life—more than a football player cherishes his Super Bowl ring; more than an auto enthusiast cherishes his hot rod; more than a Texan cherishes his freedom and his brisket; more than the gamer cherishes his shelves of precious board games; more than an old man cherishes the explosive giggles of his first grandson; more than a mother cherishes her newborn baby.

Through trust in Jesus, this is who you are right now! The holy King, Priest, and special possession of God himself! One Christian coach I know often asks his clients, "Who are you?" Like most people, they generally respond, "I am an architect or father or wife or athlete." And he tells them, "No. You are the beloved child of God, redeemed by the blood of Jesus!" That's your identity! You really are somebody special!

And here is why this is so important: Who you are shapes how you think, and how you think shapes what you do. Jesus' dear disciple John said it this way:

See what kind of love the Father has given to us, that we should be called children of God; and so we are. . . . Beloved, we are God's children now, and what we will be has not yet appeared; but we know that when he appears we shall be like him, because we shall see him as he is. And everyone who thus hopes in him purifies himself as he is pure. No one born of God makes a practice of sinning, for God's seed abides in him; and he cannot keep on sinning, because he has been born of God.

Beloved, let us love one another, for love is from God, and whoever loves has been born of God and knows God. Anyone who does not love does not know God, because God is love. In this the love of God was made manifest among us, that God sent his only Son into the world, so that we might live through him. (1 John 3:1-3,9; 4:7-9 English Standard Version [ESV])

Notice, Christian, that through Jesus, you are the child of God right now! John says that if you know and believe that, it shapes how you think. Your thoughts are purified. You begin to see the world in the way that Jesus sees the world: through his purified eyes of grace, hope, and peace. And the way you think shapes what you do. John gives us two specific examples. First of all, you no longer make a practice of sinning. That doesn't mean you become perfect. That's not possible this side of heaven. But sin is not your practice—just like an Olympic hurdler does not make a practice of knocking over the hurdles, even though it still happens from time to time. In other words, through your new identity in Jesus, your purified heart strives to love and serve God faithfully in everything. Second, you begin to love other people the way that Jesus does. Who you are shapes how you think, which, in turn, shapes what you do. I am a child of God; I think like Jesus does (in my best moments); I love God and serve others.

If you believe you are a nobody, your thoughts will continually be plagued with worry and desperate plans to become somebody. If you are confident that you are God's somebody, your thoughts will be shaped by peace and humble confidence because your status before God and your future are secure in Jesus. If you believe you are a nobody, you will always be busy seeking yourself. If you are confident that you are God's somebody, you will be busy serving God and others—especially the nobodies of the world. This is how we will approach the issue of being a nobody and a somebody in this book:

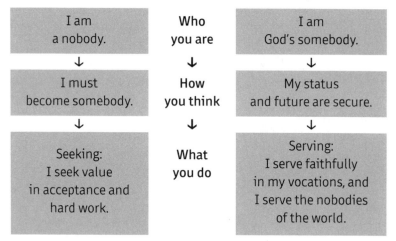

I am a nobody.	Who you are	I am God's somebody.
↓	↓	↓
I must become somebody.	How you think	My status and future are secure.
↓	↓	↓
Seeking: I seek value in acceptance and hard work.	What you do	Serving: I serve faithfully in my vocations, and I serve the nobodies of the world.

Contingency plans

Your worst-case scenario is that you end up with just God.

—Pastor Mike Novotny,
*3 Words That Will Change
Your Life*

I am guessing many of you readers already know this. Maybe you grew up in the church, went to Sunday school, said your prayers, and got confirmed or made the good confession in some other way. Maybe you went on youth group trips and attended teen Bible study regularly. Maybe you went to a Christian college or frequented your campus ministry events. Maybe you can be seen regularly at Bible studies and small groups, flipping comfortably through your dog-eared Bible and feverishly taking notes. You've literally heard hundreds of sermons. Your shelves are filled with devotional books and commentaries. You've watched all the Jesus movies and listen to Christian radio on your commute. Maybe you volunteer regularly at the church or even serve as a full-time leader.

So, yeah, maybe you've heard this all before. You don't need to read another book about who you are in Jesus.

But maybe you do. If you're anything like me (and most of that description describes me), no matter how long you've been a Christian, you are regularly (and secretly) afraid that Jesus will not be enough to truly satisfy you forever and solve the Somebody Problem once and for all. So you are regularly tempted to add something to Jesus as a contingency plan: "Jesus plus *something* equals *true* somebody-ness."

Pastor Tim Keller once counseled a Christian teenager who was upset because she felt ugly and undesirable. Pastor Keller tried to assure her that Jesus loved her and offered her true and lasting peace. Her response was very telling. She said, "But what good is that if no one will go out with you?" She seemed to trust in Jesus, but she was afraid that he would not be enough to satisfy her deepest longings. So her contingency plan for happiness was to find a boyfriend. Then she would feel like somebody—just in case Jesus was not able to get her to that point.

We are all tempted to have a fallback position, a fail-safe plan when it comes to being a somebody. Jesus is a nice set of pliers to have in life's toolkit when things aren't great, but we secretly doubt he could ever satisfy our deepest longings. I will trust Jesus to make me somebody, but just in case he can't, I'd better overstuff my savings account, maintain a hot body that turns heads, acquire a thousand little thumbs-up for every post, or be the top producer at the office every month.

But all these contingency plans only compound the stress, worry, and frustration in the long run. After all, how much monetary padding do you really need to guarantee somebody-ness? How hot of a body is hot enough, especially after 40 when the crow's-feet show up and hair starts to grow out of strange places? How many likes will guarantee your value, and what will acquire more tomorrow? And how many months in a row do you need to be on top to know you are good enough? And what happens when that new salesperson surpasses your numbers?

In the sixth century B.C., three Jewish men—Shadrach, Meshach, and Abednego—were brutalized beyond anything most of us will ever experience. They witnessed the devastation of their homeland and capital city by the merciless Babylonian army. Their loved ones and neighbors were gutted and crushed into the dust. The holy treasures of their beloved temple were hauled off like the unwanted junk left at the end of a yard sale. Because they were handsome young men with a good upbringing, they were chosen like prize cattle and hauled off into captivity to serve their conquerors. They were forced to leave their Jewish identity behind by training in all the pagan ways of their captors; they were expected to dress, talk, look, and think exactly like the people who had taken everything away from them. They were most likely castrated as they prepared for service in the royal court, according to the custom of the times (see Isaiah 39:7 and 2 Kings 20:18). Even if they returned home someday, as eunuchs they could never participate in the public worship of the temple. These men had probably been pretty high up the social ladder at home, but here in Babylon, they were nothing.

They endured the whole horrific and humiliating process with a quiet dignity. Through the work ethic and persistence that had been ingrained in them from birth, they thrived in hopeless circumstances. They even excelled to the point that they were selected for special service to the king of Babylon himself, the most powerful monarch in the world at that time. And they faithfully served him, the man who had single-handedly ruined their lives.

Until . . .

. . . they were ordered to choose between bowing down to a giant golden idol or being thrown into a blazing furnace (Daniel 3). When they adamantly refused to dishonor their God by worshiping another deity, King Nebuchadnezzar magnanimously gave them a chance to reconsider.[6] Their response is astounding:

> King Nebuchadnezzar, we do not need to defend ourselves before you in this matter. If we are thrown into the blazing furnace, the God we serve is able to deliver us from it, and he will deliver us from Your Majesty's hand. But even if he does not, we want you to know, Your Majesty, that we will not serve your gods or worship the image of gold you have set up. (Daniel 3:16-18)

Do you hear what they are saying? "We hope that our God will deliver us from the fire. But even if he does not, we are okay with that, because our God is enough for us in life and death." If anyone seemed to have a reason to doubt whether God would come through for him, it was these three men. Their God had not intervened to save their homeland from devastation. It seemed that he had ignored the desperate pleas of deliverance offered up at the holy temple that was now stripped bare. God had allowed these young men to be brutalized and serve a godless king. And yet they had no contingency plans; they didn't need them. They knew that, even if they lost the scraps they still had—even if they lost their lives—they would still have God, and that was enough for them.

What did they know about God that we don't? Why didn't they have a contingency plan for their lives?

Remember: Who you are shapes how you think, and how you think shapes what you do. You see it in these three young men. They lost everything. Not proverbially, but they *actually* lost everything—their culture, their family, their status, their manhood—yet they never forgot who they were. That's why they confidently told the most powerful man in the world, "The God we serve is able to deliver us from [the blazing furnace], and he will deliver us." They knew they were children of the one true God of power and love. They knew he

---

[6] Which, by the way, shows the incredible value the king placed on them. In those days, the king was considered god incarnate; telling him no was a recipe for instant execution.

was powerful enough to save them if he wanted. They knew he loved them and would rescue them in this life or usher them safely into the next. Either way, he would deliver them. And so they could face the fire without fear.

Who they were—God's children—shaped how they thought: "God will deliver us in this life or the next; our future is secure." And how they thought shaped what they did—they stood up to the most powerful man in the world without flinching. Maybe they were even thinking of these words written many decades before by the great prophet Isaiah:

> Now, this is what the LORD says—he who created you, Jacob, he who formed you, Israel: "Do not fear, for I have redeemed you; I have summoned you by name; you are mine. When you pass through the waters, I will be with you; and when you pass through the rivers, they will not sweep over you. When you walk through the fire, you will not be burned; the flames will not set you ablaze. For I am the LORD your God, the Holy One of Israel, your Savior." (Isaiah 43:1-3)

God had promised these three young men: "You are mine." That gave them confidence to stand up to an arrogant monarch and face the flames courageously.

Shadrach, Meshach, and Abednego were not disappointed by the God they trusted. When the Babylonian king witnessed the audacity of these young men, he was furious. Nobody spoke to him that way. He ordered the furnace cranked up seven times hotter than normal and had those poor men thrown in like kindling. He expected instant disintegration, but instead he saw four men strolling around the floor of that giant Weber grill. That's not a misprint—there were *four* men now. Jesus himself walked with them in a rare appearance before his physical birth into our world.

If these three young men had any doubt about their decision to stand with God, God now stood with them in the fire. He assured them through his gracious presence that they were somebody special to him.

It's my prayer that this book helps you truly believe that you are somebody through Jesus Christ, someone who is eternally cherished by God. It's my prayer that these beautiful truths will empower you to throw away your contingency plans and serve Christ boldly, like the poet Asaph, who wrote, "Whom have I in heaven but you? And earth has nothing I desire besides you. My flesh and my heart may fail, but God is the strength of my heart and my portion forever" (Psalm 73:25,26).

One of the members of the Ghosts of Pasha said, "When the crowd screams at you like you're The Beatles, you act like The Beatles." God tells you that you are someone special, that you are his child, his very own treasured possession, and a coheir with Christ. Only, in this case, it is not a prank—it is reality, so you can act like it.

Nobody's Fig Leaves

You know, the Stone was really not such a wonderful thing. As much money and life as you could want! The two things most human beings would choose above all—the trouble is, humans do have a knack of choosing precisely those things that are worst for them.

—Professor Dumbledore,
Harry Potter and the Sorcerer's Stone

Charlie Brown is one of the most memorable and enduring cartoon characters of all time. That fascinates me because his head is essentially an oval with two dots for eyes and a simple squiggly line where his hair should be.[7] He wears the exact same yellow shirt with a wavy black line in every comic frame, every TV special, and every movie. He's not a Rembrandt, that's for sure. But he endures. Why is that?

Charlie Brown regularly has these hopeless fantasies of becoming somebody special. Whether it is finally kicking the football that Lucy always yanks away a nanosecond before he connects or catching the eye of the little red-haired girl, he convinces himself that *this time* he will succeed. But he always fails, and he always achieves that failure in spectacular ways.

In one particular comic strip, he has been psyching himself up for a winning baseball season as the inaugural game is about to begin. He envisions his team of misfits finally achieving glory in the Little League World Series. It's so real to him that he can hear the cheers

---

[7] He's got some serious male-pattern baldness for a grade-schooler.

of the crowd and feel the pats on the back: "Good ol' Charlie Brown!" Then he steps onto the pitcher's mound and lines up. The echoes of that grand dream are still playing in his mind as he hurls the very first pitch of the season. The bat connects with the ball and drills it so hard toward Charlie Brown that it blasts off his shirt, hat, shoes, and socks while he pinwheels through the air. Charlie is left lying on the pitcher's mound in nothing but his shorts, a fitting symbol of his relentless shame and humiliation. He is a hopeless nobody, and nothing he does ever makes him feel like a somebody.

My friend Gretchen once confessed that she disliked Charlie Brown cartoons because Charlie never got a break, but that's the point. Charlie Brown has endured the decades because so many people can identify with him. We all know what it's like to feel like a shameful nobody—for weeks, months, or even years at a time. We all know what it's like to have hopeless fantasies of finally becoming successful. We all know what it's like to fail miserably. Some of us even know what it's like to succeed marvelously and still feel like a nobody.

All of us have experienced that moment when we are lying on the proverbial pitcher's mound in our boxers while the entire world looks on. Many of us have even dreamed that we are standing in front of a crowd, suddenly discovering that we are only wearing underwear.[8] That's what makes Charlie Brown so relatable. Charlie's sidekick, Linus, once said to him in an exasperated voice, "Of all the Charlie Browns in the world, you're the Charlie Browniest." Even Linus knows that Charlie's the mascot of the world's nobodies. That's why we keep going back to him.

Shame and fig leaves

But let's pause for just a moment. Why do people so easily identify with Charlie Brown? Where does this debilitating sense of shame come from? It goes all the way back to the Garden of Eden, to our very first parents, Adam and Eve. Even if you are not that familiar with the Bible, you probably know a little bit about Eve taking a bite of that forbidden fruit.

---

[8] Just me? Okay. Never mind.

God had given Adam and Eve only one command in the Garden of Eden: "Don't eat the fruit of this one tree." That seems a little picky, doesn't it? Why that tree? Why forbid them from eating any fruit at all? Was God a control freak? But it seems that this was God's way of giving Adam and Eve an out—a way to walk away from him if they chose to. He didn't want robots or slaves but partners in his creative work. That tree was a place of worship where they could say, "Today again, we choose you, God."

But they wanted more than God. They wanted to be their own gods. Somehow, the devil tricked them into thinking, *We're enslaved under God's oppressive thumb, but we can really become somebody if we emancipate ourselves.*

They already were somebody special before God, the God who had handcrafted them in love; the God who walked and talked with them as his precious children, friends, and partners in his creative labor. So when they turned away from that empowering status, they were on their own. They rebelled against their very natures. They grasped at godhood and discovered hands full of nothing.

The result was debilitating shame. Genesis 3:7 says, "Then the eyes of both of them were opened, and they realized they were naked; so they sewed fig leaves together and made coverings for themselves." Why did they finally realize that they were naked at that very moment? Was there suddenly a cold breeze in the garden? No. When they stepped from the glory of being somebody into the cesspool of rebellion, they were immediately soaked in shame. For the first time, they felt spiritually and emotionally naked, their failure and stupidity exposed to each other.

There once was a little boy who had an incredible gift of focus. Even as a baby, the boy's intense gaze could feel a bit unsettling to some. People were astounded at how focused he could be even as a grade-schooler. One time, his parents sent him upstairs to take a shower. A half hour later, they hadn't heard anything from the bathroom or the boy's bedroom, so the dad went to check on him. There he was, sitting in the middle of all his Legos, intensely building something . . .

. . . completely naked.

"Hey, buddy, why don't you have any clothes on?" The little boy slowly looked up at his dad, then slowly down at his lap, and suddenly jolted in surprise—the kind of jolt you have when you think you are alone in a room and someone unexpectedly touches you on the shoulder. He had no idea that he was naked. He was so focused on what was before him that his nakedness never entered his mind.

The idea of nakedness never even occurred to Adam and Eve until they took their focus off God's presence and love. Suddenly they looked down and realized that their failure and shame were exposed to the world. For the first time, they felt like nobody, and they were desperate to cover it up. Of course, there was no Target handy to run to for a pair of designer jeans and a nice polo. So they sewed fig leaves together in a literal attempt to cover their own butts.

"Then [they] heard the sound of the Lord God as he was walking in the garden in the cool of the day, and they hid from the Lord God among the trees of the garden" (Genesis 3:8). Even though the fig leaves seemed to provide some relief from the sense of shame between Adam and Eve, God's presence was another story! Trying to conceal their shame from him was like playing hide-and-seek with a Navy SEAL in an open field while wearing hunter orange. They didn't stand a chance.

Professor Brené Brown defines shame as the "intensely painful feeling or experience of believing we are flawed and therefore unworthy of acceptance and belonging."[9] It's more than the feeling that we've done something wrong—it's the feeling that there is something innately wrong with us. But even more than that, it is the natural response of Adam and Eve's descendants before a perfect and holy God. Adam and Eve knew that they were not worthy of God's love and acceptance in this fallen state. In fact, they were only deserving of punishment, banishment, and utter destruction—thus their lame

---

[9] Brené Brown, *I Thought It Was Just Me* (New York: Gotham Books, 2007), Kindle file, Chapter 1.

attempt to cover up the debilitating shame with fig leaves, the only clothing they could scrounge up in the garden.

Most of us, maybe all of us, understand shame, the creeping fear that there is something innately wrong with us—feelings of inadequacy, hopelessness, failure, and inferiority; heart-wrenching regret over the evil we have done or the good we have left undone; embarrassment and harassment from the evil done to us or the debilitating thoughts that poison our minds. All this makes us feel exposed before God and others, horrified that we are worthless and unlovable.

So we sew figurative fig leaves together to conceal our shame and prove that we are still somebody worthwhile. Or, to use another picture, we project a dazzling image of what we want God and other people to see, like the Wizard of Oz, while the real self hides behind a flimsy curtain, frightened and hopelessly insecure.

A pastor once counseled a couple who seemed to have the perfect life, home, and marriage. He wasn't even quite sure why they had asked him for a little help; they didn't appear to have any problems in need of counseling. But as he asked some initial questions and poked around a bit into their relational dynamics, bitterness and shame began to peel back their fig leaves one at a time, like some slow and tragic striptease. Then suddenly, without warning, a tornado of pent-up frustration tore off the remaining foliage, and the whole disastrous relationship was exposed. The husband hatefully ranted that his wife was controlling and manipulative; the wife spitefully revealed that her husband was a closet drunk. She seized a tumbler from the cupboard to illustrate just how much hard liquor he guzzled every single night.

But then, as quickly as the fig leaves had blown off, the couple gathered them up again like a kid desperately chasing his windblown homework down the street.

They simultaneously realized they had let the pastor in on the closely guarded secret that they were a mess like everyone else. Within seconds, they were back to the picture of a perfect upper middle-class couple "livin' the dream." The pastor was shocked to find himself on their doorstep, the two of them cheerfully wishing him a good evening, all smiles and thanks. The bitterness and shame were tucked away as if they had never existed, fig leaves perfectly back in place.

By nature, we are all terrified that God and others will reject us if they see what we are really like. So we believe we have to keep gluing more fig leaves onto our torso to prevent them from seeing the real us. Let them see the somebody we hope to become or, at least, the somebody we want them to *think* we have become. We promise that we will let God and other people see the real us as soon as we get our junk together, when we don't have anything to be ashamed of.

So in the next few chapters, let's examine some fig leaves, or *somebody strategies*, we use to cover up our shame when we are afraid we are nobody and are trying to become somebody again.

However, before we end this chapter, can I give you a little preview of the message of hope coming later? I hate to leave you exposed. The account of Adam and Eve's descent into nobody-ness is recorded in Genesis 3. In Genesis 1, we are introduced to the God of the universe. In the original Hebrew Bible, the word for God is *Elohim,* a name that signifies his infinite power and knowledge. As he creates the universe, the laws of physics, the stars, the atoms, the creatures, and time itself, we are reminded continually that he is *Elohim;* he is the Ultimate Power. But starting in Genesis 2, he is given a new name: "the LORD God." In the Hebrew Bible, the word translated "LORD" sounds like Yahweh, or Jehovah as some people say it today. This name comes from the Hebrew word "to be" and essentially means "He is . . ." that is, "He is" always faithful, constant, loving, unchanging. So as Adam and Eve are created in Genesis 2, we are reminded of the ultimate power *and* unchanging love of their Creator.

Now, Genesis 3 is all about their rebellion—how they become nobodies. You might expect the Bible to return to the name *Elohim* to emphasize God's power, that he can and will punish rebellion. Instead, throughout the entire chapter, he is still called "the LORD God." Though Adam and Eve were now naked and ashamed, the Lord came looking for them—not to destroy them but to assure them that his love for them had not changed, to begin to restore their somebody-ness.

In fact, at the end of this tragic chapter, God does something astonishing. Genesis 3:21 says, "The LORD God made garments of skin for Adam and his wife and clothed them." The only place that you get garments of skin is from animals, and the only way that you get their skin is to kill them. This is the very first death in the history of the world. God did not execute Adam and Eve to deal with their shame and unworthiness. Instead, he killed something else to cover their shame. An innocent animal was sacrificed so they could begin to stand with humble confidence in God's presence again.

Thousands of years later, Jesus, the *Lamb* of God, would be sacrificed on a wooden cross. He would be rejected and shamed so that you could be accepted and honored before God. He would cover you with his honorable life like a robe of righteousness so that when God looks at you through Jesus, he sees someone who is worthy of his eternal love and acceptance.

Maybe you feel like you are a nobody; maybe you are terrified to let down the fig leaves in your life. The Lord God is not coming to destroy you but to assure you, "My love for you has never changed." Through Jesus, you enter a place where you can be fully known and fully loved by the Lord God, a place where your somebody-ness is truly restored, now and forever.

Part 2

Somebody Strategies

*As I have a position in the world, keep me from making
the world my position; May I never seek in the creature
what can only be found in the Creator.*

—A Puritan Prayer

In *The Peanuts Movie,* Charlie Brown is once again desperate to win the affection of that stunning red-headed girl he has been chasing for over five decades (yet, somehow, he has never aged a day). Charlie pours out his heart to Lucy, the self-proclaimed neighborhood shrink: "Let's just say there is this girl I'd like to impress, but she's something and I'm nothing. If I were something and she was nothing, I could talk to her. Or if she was nothing and I was nothing, I could talk to her. But she's something and I'm nothing, so I just can't talk to her."

Lucy's advice is characteristically insensitive: "Look into this mirror, Charlie Brown. This is the face of failure. A classic failure face. Do you think girls like failures, Charlie Brown?" She continues, "Girls want someone with proven success. Have you won any awards? Like a congressional Medal of Honor? Or a Nobel Peace Prize? What are your real estate holdings? Do you have a diversified portfolio?" She concludes, "Let me let you in on a little secret, Charlie Brown. If you really want to impress girls, you need to show them you're a winner." So Charlie sets out to prove that he is a winner.

Can you identify? I sure can. When we are feeling like a nobody, we often set out to prove our significance, which leads to all kinds of trouble. In these next few chapters, let's explore the different methods people use to achieve somebody status and why these methods are doomed to fail.

Acceptance Junkies

I confess, a mighty fear of irrelevance drove me to this vocation, a pressing anxiety that unless you looked back at me with a smile and a nod and said, "Oh, I see you. You exist. You are real to me and to this world and we're glad you showed up," I might just wither away and die.

—Andrew Peterson,
Adorning the Dark

For so long, all I wanted was for you to love me, to accept me. I thought it was my honor that I wanted, but really, I was just trying to please you. You, my father, who banished me just for talking out of turn. My father, who challenged me, a 13-year-old boy, to an Agni Kai! How can you possibly justify a duel with a child?

—Zuko,
Avatar: The Last Airbender
Book 3: Fire

How important is a name?

The Supreme People's Court in China recently ruled that a Chinese sportswear company must stop using the Chinese characters for Michael Jordan's name. Qiaodan Sports registered the name over ten years ago without Jordan's permission. Since that time, they have printed his number 23 on their merchandise along with a silhouette of a basketball player that looks suspiciously like the Jordan logo used on Nike products—in the way that an actual photo of the US president looks suspiciously like that actual US president. They didn't even bother to change the direction of the logo or the position of its legs or anything. It's probably the most flagrant aping of a logo in the history of logos.[10]

But no longer. No, sir! Jordan told the BBC, "I am happy that the Supreme People's Court has recognized the right to protect my name. . . . Chinese consumers deserve to know that Qiaodan Sports and its products have no connection to me." He then added, "Nothing is more important than protecting your own name, and today's decision shows the importance of that principle."[11]

Okay. So Mr. Jordan is partly correct. Proverbs 22:1 does say that "a good name is more desirable than great riches; to be esteemed is better than silver or gold." But in Ephesians 1:19-21, missionary Paul references "the mighty strength [God] exerted when he raised Christ from the dead and seated him at his right hand in the heavenly realms, far above all rule and authority, power and dominion, and *every name that is invoked, not only in the present age but also in the one to come*" (emphasis mine). And he writes in Philippians 2:9-11, "Therefore God exalted [Jesus] to the highest place and gave him *the name that is above every name,* that at the name of Jesus every knee should bow, in heaven and on earth and under the earth, and every tongue acknowledge that Jesus Christ is Lord, to the glory of God the Father" (emphasis mine). Sorry, Mr. Jordan. So close, but not quite. There is something more important than protecting your own name: it's honoring the name of Jesus, the Name above all names, the King of all kings.

Honestly, I am generally more worried about honoring and protecting my own name and reputation than that of Jesus. This is how my mind works: If I am extra funny or extra interesting or extra kind or extra thoughtful, people will really like me. And if people really like me, I must be doing something right, and I must be somebody. If they speak my name to others with a hint of reverence and respect;

---

[10] Okay, maybe "Bucksstar" coffee in one Chinese city ties for the winner—with the exact same two-tailed siren logo we've all come to love or hate depending on your preference for expensive, dark-roasted coffee.

[11] After this ruling, I still saw Qiaodan sportswear for sale in China at a local mall. Oh, well. Nice try, Mr. Jordan.

if they smile when they think of me; if they like my posts and comment positively on my astute observations about all matters political, religious, literary, and popular, I must be on the right track, and I must be somebody—right? So I try extra hard to be liked—whatever it takes. I pine for that cartoony banana-colored thumbs-up that is the crack for every modern acceptance junkie.

When I am in that state of mind (more often than I care to admit), I avoid anything that might cause me to be disliked. If being liked is the yellow sun that grants me temporary superpowers, being disliked is the kryptonite I fear most. I live in almost constant fear of disappointing people and dealing with the fallout of that. Even if people are smiling to my face, I fear that they are talking about me behind my back. So I go out of my way to be extra funny, even to the point of being inappropriate. I go out of my way to flatter people or do extra favors for them, not as much out of love for them as for maintaining or regaining their love for me. How twisted is that? I even find myself driven to win the approval of people who are merely acquaintances or whom I've never even met, sometimes to the neglect of those who are close to me—all to feed the carnivorous beast of somebody-ness.

Then there are the times I should have said something to someone who was out of line or was trashing the name of another in my presence, but I didn't because I didn't want to lose his respect or endure his ire. Or I spoke when I should have been silent, making jokes at the expense of others or sharing a juicy morsel of information that would make someone else look bad and me look better.

Though people may not generally see it on the surface, I am often desperately protecting my own name instead of honoring Christ's. Instead of loving other people just to love them, I am living like a parasite on their approval to build a better name for myself. I use them to achieve my own selfish somebody ends. In fact, even writing this book is a temptation for me. I think that perhaps I may win acceptance and respect from you as you read it. Has it worked? I really want to know! Please go to my Facebook page and give me a thumbs-up. Do it now!

What a mess I am.

And then, when that *acceptance* program doesn't go as planned, I slide into self-pity, make excuses for my poor performance, blame others for my lack of acceptance, and secretly despise those who have rejected me. If people even appear to question my abilities or my decisions, I quickly scorn them in my heart or complain about them to others. I take their words and actions in the worst possible way because I am terrified that people are looking down on me. I get too upset too quickly when someone challenges me. Jesus, forgive me. Instead of honoring your name, I am too busy protecting my own.

Here's the truth: No matter how great your name and reputation are, no matter how much you are liked right now, there is no way you can please everybody, every time. At some point, you will disappoint someone. If your sense of being somebody comes from that person's acceptance, you will begin to doubt your somebody-ness—the closer that person is to you, the greater the doubt. Additionally, even if it seems like everyone likes you, your lust to feed the ravenous Sarlacc Pit[12] of acceptance will leave you regularly terrified that you are going to lose that acceptance. Instead of peace, you will have anxiety. You will say and do things you know that you shouldn't just to achieve a level of acceptance that makes you feel like somebody.

"This is me"

> *That stupid Calvin. He's so mean. All I try to do is be friends, and he treats me like I'm a nobody. Well, who needs jerks like him anyway? I don't need him for a friend. I can have fun by myself.* [In the next frame Suzie sits alone on a rock, poking at the dirt with a stick.] *Poop.*

> —Bill Watterson,
> *Calvin and Hobbes*

---

[12] Still more nerdy stuff. If you haven't watched *Star Wars: Return of the Jedi,* you might need to do that after finishing this chapter. But please finish this chapter, otherwise I won't feel accepted.

If you can't achieve acceptance from those around you, maybe you can discover it within you. If no one else really appreciates your value, maybe you just need to value yourself.

In the movie *Wayne's World,* Wayne Campbell is stalked by his former girlfriend, Stacy, who cannot get it through her head that they have broken up. When Wayne tells her for the umpteenth time to leave him alone, she does everything she can to spark his jealousy. She rustles up a new boyfriend, drags that unsuspecting sap to a party, and positions herself so that Wayne can see her passionately kissing him. She laughs a little too loudly and acts a little too happy. It's clear to Wayne and everyone else that she is faking it. But she is convinced that if Wayne sees how happy she is, he will become insanely jealous and she can win him back.

Like Stacy, many people feel like their fickle boyfriend—Acceptance—has broken up with them, that is, they feel like their attempts to achieve the acceptance of family, friends, classmates, and coworkers have failed. They are desperate to win Acceptance back, so they try a little too hard to prove that they never really needed this boyfriend anyway. If people won't accept them, well, then they will just accept themselves as they are. They are perfectly fine on their own, thank you very much.

Just consider all the self-power songs that have become so popular in the last few decades. "I am a champion, and you're gonna hear me roar" by Katy Perry; "I only wanted to get your attention But you overlooked me somehow . . . How do you like me now?" by Toby Keith; and my particular favorite, "I am brave, I am bruised, I am who I'm meant to be, this is me" from the musical *The Greatest Showman.* The message in all these lyrics is clear: "I don't need you anymore. I have moved on. I am fine on my own without you! I won't let anyone bring me down because I am me, and I am proud of who I am!"

If you can't get people to accept you or you have been rejected in some way, modern culture steps in to tell you that you are still special simply because of what's inside you. You are powerful; you can do anything. All you need to do is accept yourself and find the somebody inside.

But all this power talk just feels so forced. In the words of Shakespeare, "The lady doth protest too much, methinks." It doesn't sound like a bunch of people who are strong; it sounds like a bunch of people who are weighed down by rejection and shame but are trying to convince themselves that they're fine. Now, I am not trying to minimize their pain; I am not saying they are weaker than others. I am only saying that their approach to feeling like somebody sounds like it's not working.

Acceptance broke up with us, and now we are out to prove that we never needed him in the first place—all with the desperate desire to rouse his jealousy and get him back. The more we post power memes on social media, the more it becomes evident that we actually do not feel strong or beautiful or capable. Like Dorothy, we keep clicking our little red heels, our eyes squeezed shut with determination, only to find out that, when we open them, we are still nowhere near home. In fact, we are moving in the opposite direction at terrifying speeds. No matter how much money we spend and effort we exert to convince kids that they are special, rates of depression, self-harm, and suicide continue to climb at an alarming rate.

The blockbuster movie *The Incredibles* takes place in an alternate reality where certain humans are blessed with superpowers. Bob Parr has godlike strength; his wife, Helen, is able to stretch her body in impossible ways. They had previously been known as Mr. Incredible and Elastigirl, a superhero duo who fought crime until the US government banned all superpower activities. Two of their three children already exhibit superpowers. Violet can turn invisible and create a defensive force field. Dash has superhuman speed.

Dash is eager to stretch his legs, as you can imagine. He has a talent that every kid dreams about when they watch a Marvel movie, but his parents forbid him using his powers or participating in sports because it will be impossible to hide his gifts. At one point, when he is extra frustrated by his restrictive life, his mom reminds him in a weary voice that "everyone's special," to which Dash responds under his breath, "Which is another way of saying no one is." It's a bitter sentiment that reveals the modern playing-card house in which we reside. Society told us that we were all special, that we only needed to believe in ourselves, that we could do anything we put our minds to, that we were all one of a kind. But then, so many of us were abused, teased, disappointed, frustrated, let down, devastated, and rejected. It occurred to us that maybe we weren't as special as we had been told. Besides that, you can't tell people that they are essentially high-functioning apes with no real Creator, purpose, or destiny in one breath and then tell them that they are special in the next breath—and expect them to really believe that in the end. It's powerless, like a water hose with a kink in it.

Shel Silverstein wrote a fascinating poem called "The Voice."

> There is a voice inside of you
> That whispers all day long,
> "I feel that this is right for me,
> I know that *this* is wrong."
> No teacher, preacher, parent, friend
> Or wise man can decide
> What's right for you—just listen to
> The voice that speaks inside.

It sounds so good. Just listen to that inner voice telling you that you are somebody special, telling you what is right for you. However, I find it rather ironic that below the original publication of this poem is an illustration of a crowd of people looking up. Mr. Silverstein may have had a totally different purpose in mind for that picture, but I think it betrays our real longing for acceptance from someone or something greater than ourselves.

True acceptance

You will never find lasting acceptance by looking *around you* or *within you*. There is only one place where you can find it. Paul David Tripp puts it this way:

> You can't look horizontally for what you will get only
> vertically. . . . The person next to you is never a safe
> source of your happiness because that person is flawed

and will inevitably fail you in some way. Only God is ever a safe keeper of the security, peace, and rest of your soul. Here is the bottom line—earth will never be your savior. Earth was created to point you to the One who alone is able to give peace and rest to your searching heart. Yet today many people say they believe in God, but they shop horizontally for what can be found only vertically.[13]

True acceptance only comes from looking up, from calling out to the Great Somebody, the God about whom the psalmist says:

> For you created my inmost being;
>   you knit me together in my mother's womb.
> I praise you because I am fearfully and
>   wonderfully made; your works are wonderful,
>   I know that full well.
> My frame was not hidden from you
>   when I was made in the secret place,
>   when I was woven together in the
>   depths of the earth.
> Your eyes saw my unformed body;
>   all the days ordained for me
>   were written in your book
>   before one of them came to be. (Psalm 139:13-16)

You are somebody because that Somebody stitched you together atom by atom, strand by strand, into who he wanted you to be. God didn't slap you together like some knockoff G.I. Joe action figure you buy at Walgreens. You are a priceless work of art that he designed in eternity and then knit together in the womb.

Even more, God has given you his name. The apostle Peter said, "Salvation is found in no one else, for there is no other name under heaven given to mankind by which we must be saved" (Acts 4:12). That not only means that all other paths to God (and thus all other paths to somebody-ness) are dead ends; that's true, of course. But in

---

[13] Paul David Tripp, *New Morning Mercies: A Daily Gospel Devotional* (Wheaton, Illinois: Crossway, 2014), Kindle file, June 2.

a positive way, it also means that you, dear child of God, don't have to prove you are worthy of God's name, because God's righteous name was given to you in Jesus.

The one-child policy in China has had many devastating effects on the population and culture of China. One of these is, historically, the preference for boys over girls. Since parents were only allowed one child, many wanted a boy who could support the family when he grew up. In fact, some parents were so desperate to have a son that, if they had a daughter, they sent her off to live with other family members so they could try again for a son.[14] This has led to millions of unregistered girls who, technically, cannot go to school, get a job, or benefit from any government programs. Other parents have been so disappointed with having girls that they have given their girls names traditionally reserved for boys, like was done to my Chinese teacher. Of course, you can name your children whatever you want; God says nothing about that. But imagine being a daughter raised like that: Every time your name is spoken, you are reminded that, from the very beginning, you were not wanted.

Dear child of God, no matter what your given name, no matter what your reputation, no matter how many people like you—the name of Jesus has been given to you. His glory is your glory; his honor is your honor. There is no other name you need in order to know that you are a somebody.

Still more, the Lord has inscribed his glorious name on you, as he told the great Jewish leader Moses, "Tell Aaron and his sons [the priests], 'This is how you are to bless the Israelites. Say to them: "The LORD bless you and keep you; the LORD make his face shine on you and be gracious to you; the LORD turn his face toward you and give you peace." ' So *they will put my name on the Israelites,* and I will bless them" (Numbers 6:23-27, emphasis mine).

When I was a kid, my little sisters begged for Cabbage Patch Kids dolls one Christmas. Unfortunately, every little girl in America asked for the same thing that year. And you know how crazy some

---

[14] I know one such girl, and that rejection has dogged her for years.

parents get about buying presents during the holidays. WWF cage matches broke out at Toys "R" Us stores across the country over those limited-edition plastic orphans. Grown men and women were ripping boxes out of the hands of other grown men and women in a desperate attempt to score the quickly diminishing stock. My parents miraculously found two dolls left at a store near our home, and they had to sneak out of the store like convicts escaping Alcatraz.[15]

Then some scoundrels started selling knockoff Cabbage Patch Kids to unsuspecting parents with that crazy look of desperation in their eyes. But they weren't so clever as they thought. Though their faux dolls were nearly flawless, they forgot one key element: the designer, Xavier Roberts, put his very unique signature on the bum of each authentic orphan. Why the bum? I have no idea. But you knew you had the real thing if his personal scribbling donned the derriere of your doll.

When you were baptized into Jesus, God emblazoned his glorious name on your heart so you can know for certain that you are an authentic somebody—not some cheap knockoff. Whenever you are afraid that you are a nobody, that no one accepts you because of your shortcomings, that your name means nothing at all, remember that God's name is on you. In fact, the Lord says, "Can a mother forget the baby at her breast and have no compassion on the child she has borne? Though she may forget, I will not forget you! See, I have engraved you on the palms of my hands" (Isaiah 49:15,16). Your name is tattooed on the palms of God's hands where he can never forget you. I used to write things on my hand to help myself remember them—much to my mother's chagrin—but it didn't take more than a washing or two for the ink to fade beyond recognition. The unforgettable was forgotten with a little bit of soap. But you are scarred upon the hands of your God—quite literally, in fact, on the palms of Jesus, whose nail scars will endure into eternity. Your name

---

[15] I should point out that my father may have embellished this story a bit for effect, or I may have imagined it this way. Either way, it was a crazy time.

is protected forever in the hand of your Savior. Nothing and nobody can scratch it off or rub it out.

Somebody Status

Jesus, I my cross have taken,
All to leave and follow Thee;
Destitute, despised, forsaken,
Thou from hence my All shalt be.
Perish ev'ry fond ambition,
All I've sought or hoped or known;
Yet how rich is my condition!
God and heav'n are still mine own.

—Henry Francis Lyte,
"Jesus, I My Cross Have Taken"

Once in a while when normal people travel, they get a little taste of real status. When one of our flights was cancelled at Chicago O'Hare Airport due to inclement weather, our family had to book a different flight with United Airlines. Once in a while (not too often, thankfully), I have been waited on by a bored or bristly airline rep who has made me feel like a total nuisance, but this rep gave me her exclusive attention for nearly a half hour even though other people were getting only two or three minutes with the other reps. She tried to get me a free night in the Hilton for all my troubles as if the thunderstorms were United's fault. Over and over again, she said variations of "I'm sorry, sir. We want to take care of you." At one point she said, "I've found a flight tomorrow, but I'm trying to get you something better." Then United gave us food vouchers for the whole family because we were inconvenienced by changing flights. The next day, we were even ushered through the premier access security line in five minutes while the other plebeians were lined up for miles.

It finally dawned on me at some point that she thought I was a United Premier Gold member because I was traveling on someone else's frequent flyer miles; a member at our church had used his own miles to purchase tickets for my whole family.

As golden as I was with United under my friend's name, I was on my own at the Hilton. Just plain ol' Matt. No premier access there. In fact, when I went to use the hotel fitness room—one of the nicest I have seen—the attendant was very eager to assist me until he typed my name into the computer. He made a face like he had just drunk an entire bottle of warm, flat soda with little bits of cottage cheese, and then he told me it would cost me $15 to use the facilities. After all, I am only a Blue level Hilton Honors guy instead of a Gold level. Back to the words of that classic 1980s movie *Can't Buy Me Love:* I went from "totally chic to totally geek" within seconds. I wanted to tell him, "I'm Gold premier access at the airport, buddy, so I belong in your fancy weight room." But I'm just a nobody. Who am I to really expect somebody status?

Our modern world is obsessed with status: who's in and who's out; who's hip and who's not; who has access; who knows whom; who's beautiful and fashionable—who's really somebody. Thankfully, in Christ we have status that far outweighs them all, but it often doesn't look like it. Actually, it often appears that the only real losers are those who put their trust in Christ, like Asaph said in Psalm 73, "The wicked get by with everything; they have it made, piling up riches. I've been stupid to play by the rules; what has it gotten me? A long run of bad luck, that's what—a slap in the face every time I walk out the door" (verses 12-14, *The Message*).

The problems of status

If you want to understand the true status of belonging to Jesus, you need to look deeper than the who's who of the world. We see that in the life of the great missionary Paul. Paul knew about status. His Jewish family had been granted Roman citizenship—something restricted to those born into it, those who could pay big money for it, or those who had rendered some exceptional service to the Roman emperor. Paul's father also sent him from Turkey to Israel to study at the feet of Gamaliel, one of the most famous Jewish religious leaders of his day. Even when Paul was languishing in jail for two years, the Roman governor kept sending for him, expecting a bribe of some sort. Paul obviously had money and connections, at least at certain times in his life.

And yet he wrote this to the Philippian Christians: "Whatever were gains to me I now consider loss for the sake of Christ. What is more, I consider everything a loss because of the surpassing worth of knowing Christ Jesus my Lord, for whose sake I have lost all things. I consider them garbage, that I may gain Christ" (Philippians 3:7,8). And later in the same letter: "I know what it is to be in need, and I know what it is to have plenty. I have learned the secret of being content in any and every situation, whether well fed or hungry, whether living in plenty or in want" (Philippians 4:12). Even though Paul was used to premier status and could have demanded privileges at different times, it meant nothing compared to Christ.

This is illustrated poignantly in the account of his time in the Philippian jail cell (Acts 16). When Paul encountered a slave girl who was demon-possessed and exploited by her owners as a fortune-teller, he cast out the demon and set her free. Her owners were furious that they had suddenly and completely lost their convenient source of income. They dragged Paul and his companion, Silas, before the city magistrates. Since both Paul and Silas were Roman citizens, it was illegal to flog them and throw them into jail without a trial. They probably weren't given an opportunity to appeal to their premier member status, or the magistrates didn't believe them. So they were flogged and thrown into jail. Then the jailer, who appeared to have been a bit of a brute who loved his job a little too much, locked them in the deepest part of the jail and fastened their feet in the stocks to render them as miserable as possible.

And yet Paul and Silas weren't sulking or sobbing in their cell; they weren't busy writing letters of appeal or plotting the demise of the magistrates. They were praying and singing songs with such genuine hope that all the other inmates and even the jailer himself were listening intently.

Why did Paul and Silas handle their difficulties so well? Because they treasured the eternal status of belonging to Christ infinitely more than Roman citizenship and an easy life.

All of us want to have premier status, to feel like we are somebody important. It's glorious to be a United Premier Gold access member once in a while; it feels great to receive kudos and be the object of everyone's affections. But you *already are* privileged, you *already are* somebody. You are a child of God, and Christ is your brother. Christ grants us the ultimate status. Anything less than him will never satisfy us enough, which is why pursuing status outside of him (as a substitute for him) leads to a continual restlessness.

There is an episode of the TV show *Frasier* that ingeniously captures this restlessness. The two pretentious brothers, Frasier and Niles, bamboozle their way into a new, exclusive health spa in their city. They are totally happy with their experience until they realize that there is a golden door behind which only certain members are ushered into greater delights. Once they schmooze their way into that level, they are content there until they see a platinum door. In an attempt to convince himself and Niles that they should be content with what they already have, Frasier says: "This is heaven, right here and now; why do we have to think about someplace else?" With longing in his voice and greed in his eyes, Niles responds, "This is only heaven for the people who can't get into the real heaven . . . the platinum heavens." Frasier weakly pleads, "Why must we allow the thought of something that at this point can only be incrementally better ruin what is here and now?" In a near panic, Niles retorts, "I don't know. Let's figure it out on the other side!" In a mad rush, they burst through the platinum door and find themselves in a back alley, locked out of the spa, with Niles wrapped like a mummy, his face covered in an exotic honey-butter beauty mask.

No matter what we attain, someone always has more. There's always a newer phone, a better model, a younger lover. And even if you get the newest and the best, that doesn't satisfy either. Solomon had more money, more sex, and more experiences than any of us will ever have in ten lifetimes, and his conclusion was that, outside of God, it was "meaningless, a chasing after the wind" (Ecclesiastes 1:14). And yet by nature it seems we can't stop seeking status. Once in a while we attain contentment in one area only to lose it in another—whether money, reputation, looks, or VIP access.

Additionally, human privilege tempts us to divide the world into who's in and who's out so that we are continually tempted to envy and criticize those with greater status while peering down on those with lesser status. Think back to missionary Paul in Philippi. How could two successful businessmen justify enslaving a demon-possessed girl to make money? How could a jailer justify torturing two men whose only crime was compassion to a slave? Because human status puts everybody on a ladder of value, obviously slaves and prisoners are less valuable than us.

This ladder is almost inescapable for us. Even if we consider our-selves to be open, unbigoted people, there are those people groups, family members, or coworkers we think are beneath us, who just aren't as dedicated or focused or generous as we are. We think, *Why can't these people just . . . ?* (You fill in the blank.) But we rarely remem-ber how much of our earthly status and how much of what we are is shaped by where and when we were born.

I love how comic Jim Gaffigan says it: "I'm tired of people acting like they're better than McDonald's. You may have never set foot in McDonald's but you have your own 'McDonald's.' Maybe instead of buying a Big Mac, you read *US Weekly.* Hey, that's still McDonald's; it's just served up a little different. Maybe your McDonald's is telling yourself that Starbucks Frappuccino is not a milkshake. . . . It's all McDonald's." We are all tempted to look down on someone; that's the damnable downside to earthly status that is not tempered by our heavenly status.

Gospel status and blessings

About midnight Paul and Silas were praying and singing hymns to God, and the other prisoners were listening to them. Suddenly there was such a violent earthquake that the foundations of the prison were shaken. At once all the prison doors flew open, and everyone's chains came loose. The jailer woke up, and when he saw the prison doors open, he drew his sword and was about to kill himself because he thought the prisoners had escaped. But Paul shouted, "Don't harm yourself! We are all here!" (Acts 16:25-28)

When a miraculous earthquake broke the chains on Paul and Silas and flung open the doors of the jail, that bully jailer was about to kill himself. He didn't want to deal with the shame and punishment of letting prisoners escape; he couldn't stand the thought of being a failure. But before he could plunge the sword into his belly, Paul shouted, "Don't harm yourself! We are all here!"

The broken man responded, "What must I do to be saved?" (Acts 16:30). This man now recognized that he was a hopeless nobody without the God that Paul and Silas sang about. However, like all people by nature, this man assumed he would have to do something good to get right with this God, to really be accepted. But Paul simply responded, "Believe in the Lord Jesus, and you will be saved" (verse 31), and then invited this man's entire household to embrace the good news of Jesus. It's reminiscent of Isaiah 55:1,2: "Come, all you who are thirsty, come to the waters; and you who have no money, come, buy and eat! Come, buy wine and milk without money and without cost. Why spend money on what is not bread, and your labor on what does not satisfy? Listen, listen to me, and eat what is good, and you will delight in the richest of fare." That's the open invitation of the gospel, the good news about Jesus Christ!

From salesperson to slave, from mindless brute to missionary, God's grace is offered freely to all because the King of all things became a backwoods Jewish peasant with no human status in order to do everything we needed to be called the children of God. It was a tragic story that ended with our premier-status Savior being counted with the executed criminals whose bodies were tossed carelessly on Jerusalem's garbage heap.

However, when we read about that earthquake in Philippi, how it shook the foundations of the prison and broke those chains, we can't help but think of another earthquake—the earthquake on Easter morning that shattered our chains of sin, death, and Satan forever when Christ rose from the dead. Because Jesus gave up his status and was raised from the dead, we are privileged to be exalted with him and enter the family of God.

There are countless wonderful blessings of this gospel status. Let me mention just a few here. First, true contentment. During another imprisonment Paul wrote to the Christians in Philippi, "I have learned to be content whatever the circumstances. I know what it is to be in need, and I know what it is to have plenty. I have learned the secret of being content in any and every situation, whether well fed or hungry, whether living in plenty or in want. I can do all this through him who gives me strength" (Philippians 4:11-13). Some skeptics say that faith in Christ is a simplistic answer to life, but that couldn't be further from the truth. Notice that belief in Jesus didn't exempt Paul and Silas from suffering. Faith wasn't a get-out-of-jail-free card as some health-and-wealth preachers would have us believe. Christ wasn't a magic charm for the inconveniences of their lives but their constant companion throughout them. Everyone experiences disappointment, pain, and trouble, no matter how privileged they are, but the child of God has every reason to face them all with contentment.

Another result of gospel status is "Jesus goggles." Because we ended up flying standby on an alternate flight the United rep found for us, we were the last people to board the plane. Our family of five was scattered throughout the seats. With the exception of you Chatty Cathys out there, most of us just want to be left alone while we travel. It's not that we're rude; we are just trying to get from point A to point B while sitting uncomfortably close to total strangers, politely trying to decide the entire flight who should have his elbow on the armrest. Case in point: The most my seatmate said to me the entire flight was

"Want a mint?" as we were deplaning, leaving me to wonder if she had been enduring my foul ham-and-Swiss breath the entire time.

My daughter, Maddie, however, sat next to a young man who looked like he had just walked out of a hippie commune. He had been all over the world. He was a free spirit. He was reading the Qur'an. Maddie struck up a conversation with him and shared her faith in Jesus, leaving him with an invitation to visit our church sometime. As we left the plane, my wife, Christine, told me, "I feel bad. I just saw a hippie; Maddie saw a soul."

When we really understand gospel status, we put on Jesus goggles. We don't see clothing, classes, or color. We see souls who need and have Jesus' love just like us. We begin to marvel that God would choose people like us to know his amazing grace. Why out of seven billion people should we be elected as the privileged, eternal children of God? I have no idea, but we are! And we have the marvelous assignment of welcoming everyone into that family. "Hey, if God accepts people like me, then, brother, you're golden!"

When gymnast Gabby Douglas won gold in the 2012 Olympics, she said, "I give all the glory to God. It's kind of a win-win situation. The glory goes up to him, and the blessings fall down on me." She doesn't see herself as better than others but blessed by God. She has Jesus goggles. It's a fine way to live! Whether we succeed or fail, we have Christ. We realize how privileged we are that Jesus should give so much to people like us!

Next time you are stuck in coach, gazing longingly through the crack between those cobalt blue curtains at the business-class patrons nom-nomming their Häagen-Dazs dulce de leche ice cream, remember your gospel status. In God's computer, you are United Gold.

Productive Somebodies

Ah, come on, Adrian, it's true. I was nobody. But that don't matter either, you know? 'Cause I was thinkin', it really don't matter if I lose this fight. It really don't matter if this guy opens my head, either. 'Cause all I wanna do is go the distance. Nobody's ever gone the distance with Creed, and if I can go that distance, you see, and that bell rings and I'm still standin', I'm gonna know for the first time in my life, see, that I weren't just another bum from the neighborhood.

—Rocky Balboa, *Rocky*

Growing up, I lived in a suburb of Chicago, and I was fiercely proud of the Windy City. On every trip down the Kennedy Expressway and through the Loop on our way to Grandma's house, I gawked through the window of our wood-paneled station wagon. I forgot all about Mom's homemade trail mix[16] for the moment as I marveled at each shimmering tower of glass rising like an angular giant from the bustle of downtown. I didn't even notice the perpetual carsickness that plagued me when I did anything in the vehicle besides stare straight ahead in a catatonic-like trance. I was in awe.

---

[16] Mom's homemade trail mix was lovingly thrown together to keep us kids busy for five minutes on a road trip before the inevitable sibling meltdown. My (sometimes) co-oping granola mother tried to keep it healthy by mixing in a variety of snacks with the coveted M&Ms. Those "melt in your mouth, not in your hands" chocolate spheres were the first to go, of course, followed by the peanuts and raisins, and then the other nuts. We left the sesame sticks for the Lake Michigan seagulls, assuming that my mom had picked them up at a pet store anyway.

Then the pièce de résistance came into view: the Sears Tower. It was a titan among the towers. Nothing compared to that black colossus with its soaring white antennae. I forgot all the other towers when we drove past it. It was the tallest building in the world at that time, a title it held for nearly 25 years. I thought it made the Empire State Building look like a rickety toy shack that Godzilla would crush in those hokey Japanese films. When you stood on the observation deck, pedestrians on the sidewalk looked like ants. The cars looked like tiny, plastic models you could pick up and throw across the city. Nothing compared with the Sears Tower.

It wasn't until much later, especially after I moved to Asia, that I realized the significance of the modern skyscraper. Since my childhood, many other cities and corporations have attempted to build their own "tower that reaches to the heavens" (Genesis 11:4). In fact, the poor Sears Tower isn't even in the top 20 list of the world's tallest buildings nowadays.[17] Building monstrous skyscrapers isn't just a means of providing office space for companies in the cramped confines of a modern city—it's a testament to the glory of humanity. Their dominating shadows proclaim, "We are wealthy; we are accomplished; we are gods."

Thankfully, Christians don't believe in that sort of thing, do we? We are all about the glory of God! Ahem . . . *awkward silence.* Take the citizens of Amiens and Beauvais, for example.

In A.D. 1220, the citizens of Amiens, France, decided to build a cathedral that would be large enough to fit all ten thousand of their townspeople at one time. They believed that the grandeur of a cathedral could glorify God and bring people closer to him . . . AND gain some glory points for their city while they were at it. Not to be outdone, the people of Beauvais, a city just 38 miles away, began to build their own cathedral—a larger, more beautiful edifice than their neighbors'. On record, both cathedrals measured 144 units high. But the builders at Beauvais were tricky: Instead of using the Roman

---

[17] It's now known as the Willis Tower. I guess Sears didn't want it anymore after it lost its title. You're still amazing to me, Lady!

foot to measure the height, they used the slightly longer royal foot. As a result, they had technically built the tallest cathedral on earth at the time.

But at what cost? During construction in 1284, part of the roof collapsed. On Ascension Day in 1573, stones began to fall from the ceiling as the clergy processed through the church. The solemn line of solemn men picked up the pace. More stones fell. The group ended up rushing out of the cathedral in a cloud of dust, like Indiana Jones fleeing a booby-trapped cave with a golden idol. To this day, the cathedral is unfinished and modern braces keep disaster from repeating itself.

It stands as a gothic monument to the arrogance and danger of human-glory projects done in the name of God.

Crumbling cathedrals

The gospel of Luke tells us about a wealthy man who had, in another sense, also successfully completed a self-glory project but found himself crumbling on the inside.

> Jesus entered Jericho and was passing through. A man was there by the name of Zacchaeus; he was a chief tax collector and was wealthy. He wanted to see who Jesus was, but because he was short he could not see over the crowd. So he ran ahead and climbed a sycamore-fig tree to see him, since Jesus was coming that way. (Luke 19:1-4)

Nobody could accuse Zacchaeus of being a slouch. He might have been a "wee little man" according to the old Sunday school song, but he got results. He wasn't just a tax collector; he was the *chief* tax collector in one of the most important trade centers of the region. He had made so much dough that when his life was changed by Jesus and he decided to return the money to those he had cheated, he offered them four times what he had extorted in the first place. This businessman had cash and power. What else could a guy want?

But think of what he had to give up to get there. He had betrayed his own people by toiling for the hated Roman Empire. The Romans didn't care how tax collectors got their cut of the taxes; they just wanted their money and no problems. So tax collectors were known for gouging people by adding exorbitant fees on top of already burdensome tax rates.

How could a man be so calloused toward his own people, the brothers and sisters with whom he had worshiped and celebrated religious festivals? Maybe it was a sense of inferiority. If you were a short guy in those days, you were *really* short. Maybe his parents rejected him or his wife left him for another man; maybe the other boys picked on him in synagogue school. Maybe he started out trying to do the right thing but fell in with bad characters and lost his way. Regardless, he seemed to think that accomplishment and the subsequent wealth would make him feel like somebody. He figured people would respect him if he succeeded, despite the way he succeeded. Or maybe he didn't really care at all what his own people thought of him; maybe he was after the respect of the powerful Romans. In any event, he tried to become somebody through what he accomplished.

Quite obviously, it had failed. Zacchaeus had struggled, scraped, and swindled to feel successful and respected by God, his associates, those who rejected him—who knows—but it was all a lie. So this creep who had probably once thought of himself as a dignified businessman was climbing trees like Tom Sawyer just to get a glimpse of the one person who might be able to address his problem: Jesus Christ.

It is important to recognize that there is nothing wrong with being an employee of the IRS; nor is there anything wrong with working for a foreign entity; nor is there anything intrinsically wrong with making boatloads of money. Zacchaeus' *motivation* is what got him into trouble. He had built a crumbling cathedral of self instead of God's glorious cathedral.

And that's where I get into trouble. I may not look anything like that swindler Zacchaeus, but I've got my own motivation problems. It's quite easy to say, "To God be the glory!" It's another thing to actually live for his glory. How much of the sweat on my brow is the result of building a glorious cathedral to myself?

Perhaps you are somebody because of your unparalleled skill, your outstanding achievements, or your strenuous work ethic. But maybe you got where you did in ways that were unwise, unkind, or even illegal. Or maybe you did it all by the book, but your driving motivation was living in the right neighborhood, driving the right car, or sending your kids to the right school so that people would respect you. You overworked: early morning commutes, late-night meetings, weekends in the office. There was always some excuse why you couldn't take your spouse on that long-overdue date. While your child brimmed with imaginative stories and a thousand questions, your mind was puzzling out office problems. You may as well have been on Saturn while he was chatting your ear off. Ten texts from your best friend went unanswered while you dealt with *real life*. Your parents asked why you rarely call or visit, but it only triggered annoyance; don't they have anything to do? You did what you felt you had to do to build the tallest tower or the most captivating cathedral, but now the ceiling is starting to collapse on the wounded nobodies left in your wake—spouse, children, parents, coworkers, or friends. Whether in ways crooked or straight, dishonest or honest, you weren't building God's glorious cathedral but your own crumbling cathedral of self. And other people ended up getting emotionally and spiritually scarred—sometimes for their entire lives.

Ministry somebodies

The robe of Christian ministry cloaks many a shameless idolatry.

—Bockmuehl, *Philippians,* p. 80,
quoted in Ben Witherington's
Commentary on Philippians, p. 82

While we are on the topic of building cathedrals, permit me to take a moment to speak to my fellow church workers who dedicate countless hours to public ministry every month. There is a special danger for us in trying to become somebody by what we do. If you are not a church worker, I encourage you to read this section also so you have some idea how to help your pastors, missionaries, and other full-time church leaders.

In the movie *Kung Fu Panda,* poor Master Shifu cannot find any peace. He tries to meditate. He chants the mantra "Inner peace, inner peace" over and over again, but nothing changes. There is no peace for him. He just has too much on his mind. There are too many setbacks and insurmountable odds, and nothing is going the way it is supposed to go—at least in the way he had always envisioned things going. Worst of all, his vicious enemy is arriving any day, and his student, the chubby panda Po, is much better at eating almond cookies than learning kung fu.

Dear church worker, maybe your life feels like that sometimes. It's difficult to live with inner peace. There is so much to do every week. There are sermons to write, couples to counsel, classes to teach, visits to make, events to plan, volunteers to coordinate, meetings to facilitate. There are wandering sheep, prickly members, and worries about finances. There are unmet expectations that you put on yourself and others put on you. There are setbacks and disappointments. All those plans you made and that wonderful ten-year vision you were so excited about—everything seems like it might implode if you don't keep swinging from tree to tree like those fidgety primates at the zoo. There is so much more that could be done and so much that could be done better, but there are often mental, spiritual, and even physical roadblocks to these important tasks you are trying to accomplish. In the center of that cyclone, you try to have inner peace, but it just will not come to you, at least not as often as you would like.

When we cannot find inner peace, it is often because we are trying to do God's work. I do not mean the ministries we have been assigned; I mean the work that only God can do. Charles Spurgeon once wrote: "You are meddling with Christ's business, and neglecting your own when you fret about your lot and circumstances." A few years ago, I learned this interesting Latin phrase: *"irreligiosa solicitudo pro Deo,"* translated as "a blasphemous anxiety to do God's work for him." How often have we blasphemed God by fretting about what only he can control?

Many of us use public ministry as a way to feel like somebody. Let's face it: People who enter the public ministry struggle with the need to be respected, accepted, affirmed, and accomplished just like everybody else. As Paul David Tripp likes to say, church workers are just as much in the middle of their sanctification as the people they minister to. Not all their motives for serving in the church are altruistic. That's why, when a church member asks how we are doing, many of us immediately respond, "I am *so* busy. No time to think. I have three meetings tonight, a sermon to write on Saturday, eight people to counsel, a conference to prep for, and I am writing a book on the side." What we are really saying is "Can't you see how busy I am? That proves that I am somebody important, doesn't it? Please, validate me! Remind me that I have value, that my work is making a difference."

In his sermon series entitled "He Covers Our Shame," Pastor Beau Hughes describes how he used sports and later public ministry as a way to deal with his shame, the conviction that he was worthless.

> Of course I was so committed to practicing and so committed to winning, because it wasn't just winning a game; it wasn't just competing; it was covering my shame. So I'm going to be driven until I drive myself to death if that's what it takes to not have to experience this fear, to not have to experience this embarrassment, to not have to experience this sense of vulnerability and nakedness. . . . Even after I became a Christian and then a Christian pastor, I continued to cover my shame with my performance. . . . Christianity and even Christian ministry became just another arena for me to achieve in, just another arena through my good works and my hard work for me to cover over my shame. And you know what? In a lot of ways, I was able to excel at it. . . . I just took that same competitiveness . . . and I brought it into the ministry.

Can you identify with that? So often, we dispensers of Jesus' undeserved acceptance fall into the trap of earning the acceptance of God and others through our deeds, hoping that our achievements will cover up our feelings of shame and inadequacy. It might be ministry work, but it's salvation through works, nonetheless. We hope that ministry will make us feel like somebody.

It's not God-pleasing, no matter what the outward results. It doesn't matter how many more people attend worship than last year, how many pack in for our Bible classes, or how many 70-hour work weeks we can pull off in a row if it's done primarily to build the crumbling cathedral of self or to cover our shame and make us feel like somebody.

Praise God that he still uses idolatrous ministry for good, just like he once used a donkey to speak his truth, but we ourselves are not flourishing through it. Church workers who neglect the faith of their family for the glory of one more baptized soul will still be able to rejoice how God brought that soul to faith, but they will also suffer the natural consequences of those who neglect their family, regardless of their vocation. Church workers who neglect their own time to rest in God because the ministry must go on—like fatally wounded medics bleeding out on their battlefield patients—may still help some fellow Christians, but they themselves will not flourish in it. Building the cathedral of self is sin, plain and simple, no matter what the results look like. The resignation of several famous and *successful* pastors in the last few years should make that abundantly clear.

Missionary Paul writes in 1 Corinthians 3:10-13:

> By the grace God has given me, I laid a foundation as a wise builder, and someone else is building on it. But each one should build with care. For no one can lay any foundation other than the one already laid, which is Jesus Christ. If anyone builds on this foundation using gold, silver, costly stones, wood, hay or straw, their work will be shown for what it is, because the Day will bring

it to light. It will be revealed with fire, and the fire will test the quality of each person's work.

Like the townsfolk of Amiens and Beauvais, we can *say* that we are building the kingdom for God's glory, but does our work highlight his efforts or ours? Do we make decisions based upon what will be best for ministry or our reputation, what is best for people or for covering our shame and making us feel like somebody again?

Missionary Paul gives us an amazing model to follow in Philippians 1:15-18:

> It is true that some preach Christ out of envy and rivalry, but others out of goodwill. The latter do so out of love, knowing that I am put here for the defense of the gospel. The former preach Christ out of selfish ambition, not sincerely, supposing that they can stir up trouble for me while I am in chains. But what does it matter? The important thing is that in every way, whether from false motives or true, Christ is preached. And because of this I rejoice.

Paul has absolutely no concern for his reputation or his control of the ministry. His competitors were preaching Christ "out of envy and rivalry." These are the same words he uses in the lists of Romans 1:29 and Galatians 5:20,21 to speak of the depravity of those who continue to run away from God. In 1 Timothy 6:4, Paul uses these words to describe false teachers. In other words, Paul's assessment of his rivals is not couched in polite Christian-ese. He labels them for what they are. And yet he says, "What does it matter? The important thing is that in every way, whether from false motives or true, Christ is preached. And because of this I rejoice." Paul, don't you realize that these bozos are making you look bad? They are telling people that you aren't a good missionary, that you must be doing something wrong to get yourself arrested for crimes against the state. Don't they realize that you are writing books of the Bible? Don't they know about the dozens of congregations in Greece and Asia Minor that have popped up because of your faithful work? Don't they know how much you have suffered for the sake of the Savior? Don't you care about your reputation, Paul?

Nope. He only cared that the good news about Jesus Christ was proclaimed throughout the world. He honestly didn't care how it happened but *that* it happened. He didn't care who knew about his important role in the work, as long as the work kept moving forward. Who cared if he was a nobody in this critical mission work as long as the name of the Great Somebody was proclaimed from the mountaintops? And who cared if people spit when they spoke Paul's name, if only their hearts quickened when they heard the name of Jesus? Lord, please give us, your public ministers, this heart that is so confident in the accomplishments of Jesus for us that it cares not if our accomplishments are forgotten forever.

So what *can* we do? We can preach the gospel. We can spend time with people and listen to them. We can pray. We can make some plans and do our best to carry them out. What can we *not* do? We cannot change people's hearts. We cannot make the ministry go faster than God and circumstances will allow. We cannot make God do what we want him to do, what we think is best for his church. He is God; he knows what is best. It is not our business to run the world and make all things work out for the good of the church. Our business is to trust and work out our vocations in that trust. God will take care of the rest.

Rebuilding the foundation

Construction on the Leaning Tower of Pisa began in A.D. 1173. After the first five years of construction, while the builders were working on the second floor, the new tower began to sink because it only had a 3-meter foundation set into weak, unstable subsoil. However, the crews just kept working on it as is until the tower was completed almost two hundred years later. In fact, in order to compensate for the tilt, the upper floors of the tower were erected with one side higher than the other. As a result, the tower is actually curved.

In 1990 it was closed to the public because of concern that it would tip over. Engineers have used cables and lead counterweights to hold it up. They have shifted the ground to stabilize it. They have slanted it slightly more upright with massive renovations. They have removed the heavy bells to reduce the weight—all of which could have been avoided if they had just started over five years into the building process and built a better foundation.

Maybe it's the time in our lives to stop the frantic construction of the crumbling cathedral of self. Maybe it's time to rebuild our foundation, a foundation standing on something infinitely more solid than self. That's what Zacchaeus was moved to do.

> When Jesus reached the spot [where Zacchaeus was perched in the tree], he looked up and said to him, "Zacchaeus, come down immediately. I must stay at your house today." So he came down at once and welcomed him gladly.
> All the people saw this and began to mutter, "He has gone to be the guest of a sinner."
> But Zacchaeus stood up and said to the Lord, "Look, Lord! Here and now I give half of my possessions to the poor, and if I have cheated anybody out of anything, I will pay back four times the amount."
> Jesus said to him, "Today salvation has come to this house, because this man, too, is a son of Abraham. For the Son of Man came to seek and to save the lost." (Luke 19:5-10)

Jesus invited himself over to Zacchaeus' house because he knew that Zacchaeus would never dream of inviting Jesus. This shunned shorty would have assumed that no respectable rabbi such as Jesus would be caught dead in the home of a traitorous tax collector. It was a nearly unsalvageable PR disaster in the making. "All the people . . . began to mutter, 'He has gone to be the guest of a sinner'" (19:7). This was another of Jesus' apparent blunders in a long list of cultural and religious faux pas that would usher in his execution.

But Jesus didn't give two hoots about PR. Banqueting with this individual sinner probably cost Jesus dozens of followers. He didn't mind. He had come "to seek and to save the lost." He proudly built Zacchaeus as a living stone into God's glorious cathedral. As Zacchaeus discovered himself set upon the solid foundation of the gracious Savior, he abandoned the crumbling cathedral of self. He no longer had any need to prove himself, to make himself acceptable. He was already loved, forgiven, and accepted by the Architect of the universe.

Maybe it's time to let your crumbling cathedral just collapse. I don't mean that you should stop working hard or quit your job. But maybe it's time to rebuild from the foundation, from the Savior who said at your baptism, "Today salvation has come to this house." He will be your motivation, your strength, and your acceptance.

The Pressure
of Performance

*My drive in life comes from a fear of being mediocre. That
is always pushing me. I push past one spell of it and discover myself as a special human being but then I feel I
am still mediocre and uninteresting unless I do something
else. Because even though I have become somebody, I still
have to prove that I am somebody. My struggle has never
ended and I guess it never will.*

—Madonna,
quoted by Tim Keller in
The Freedom of Self-Forgetfulness,
Kindle file, Chapter 1

The young man told his father that he often pictured the entire
world as a stage. Sometimes other people were on the stage while he
looked on. Sometimes he was on the stage while the audience stared
up at him. They critically evaluated his every move, good and bad,
his successes and his failures. Sometimes they cheered; sometimes
they clapped; sometimes they stood silently in judgment. Then the
young man teared up. "You know how in those old movies, when they
would pull someone off the stage with a cane? Well, it's like God is
standing offstage. Only he's holding a noose instead of a cane." At
this point he began to sob as he told his father that he was afraid that
one day he would make his last mistake and God would drag him off
the stage in that noose. He quoted the Bible verse that says, "How
suddenly are they destroyed, completely swept away by terrors!"

(Psalm 73:19). He related many of the ways he thought he had failed on that stage—some incidents more recently, some years before.

Oh, the pressure of performance! In our culture, in the church and out of it, we keep telling each other (especially our kids) that you can do anything you want to do. It's the theme of nearly every Disney movie ever made in the last few decades. It's woven into the fabric of our public education system; sometimes it seems like it's the more important intended outcome than proficiency in reading, writing, and arithmetic. It's meant to empower kids, but it often ends up crippling them. After all, according to that sentiment, if they ever fail at something, they really only have themselves to blame—even if it wasn't their fault or the results were completely beyond their control. We told them that they can do anything they want to. But the reality is, if you are 5'2" and 110 pounds, you will never play in the NFL, no matter how much you set your heart on it. It quite often just messes with their minds and hearts. The result is that some kids grow up only to give up, choosing to be heroes of imaginary worlds instead of facing the prospect of failure in the real one. Other kids grow up to be workaholics, defined not only as those who work really hard but as those who define themselves by their success (or lack of it), who seek value through what they do.

This pressure of performance drives many of us to boast in the flimsy plastic trophies of the past. This one brags about the winning three-pointer in high school 20 years ago; that one can still do one-armed push-ups; this one still holds the highest PR (personal record) at the gym; that one's curves can still turn a young guy's head; this one surpassed 1500 on her SAT 15 years ago—and on and on. Under the pressure of performance, we often parade any little accomplishment we can find to assure ourselves that we've still got it—all while we feel significance slipping away.

The pressure of performance is a relentless slaver in the present. In a desperate effort to distance ourselves from the descending noose of judgment—the judgment we feel from God, others, or our own hearts—we often dance ourselves into a frenzy. We live in a nearly constant fear of dropping even one of the countless fragile burdens we carry. We think (and sometimes say), "If I don't do *X*, who is gonna do it? If I don't continue *X*, everything is going to fall apart." The constant pressure plagues our emotions, our health, and our spirit. We're short-tempered and short on sleep. We self-medicate with antacids, alcohol, Oreos, and late-night binge TV. We rush through our time with God or skip it altogether—maybe we will get to it when things slow down a bit.

The pressure of performance fetters us for the future. With the passion of a doomsday prophet, our hearts predict imminent disaster, leaving us wide awake at two in the morning, YouTubing in a desperate attempt to shut our brains down and get back to sleep. We suffer from anticipatory anxiety as we ruminate over that upcoming meeting, that possible layoff, that struggling kid. We are exhausted before we ever face the actual event that has tangled our stomach and our thoughts up in knots.

Mindlessly following the crowd

One of the many reasons we wither under the pressure of performance is that we often uncritically follow the crowd, learning to value what others value simply because they value it. The Irish folk group The High Kings captures this well in "On the One Road," a classic ditty about an army marching aimlessly through the countryside. The soldiers don't have a clue where they are marching to or even if they are marching in the right direction, but they don't mind because at least they are marching together. It's comforting; it's affirming—unless you're walking into the trap of an enemy.

People often filter their life choices through this lens: "I would rather be somebody on the way to nowhere than a nobody on the way to anywhere." Shortly after I shared the gospel with a certain Chinese lady, she responded by informing me about her culture's traditional ancestral practices, such as worshiping dead relatives and all the ritual details involved in that. It was as if she was trying to convince herself that she must be in the right group; after all, there were so many people in her group and her group had a centuries-long heritage. What could be wrong with that? Even though the gospel clearly tugged at her heart, she sought safety in the group instead. She would rather be a somebody doing her thing in the group even if it's going the wrong way than feel like a nobody alone on the way to heaven.

Being somebody in the group makes many people feel like they are spiritually and emotionally safe. After all, how could so many people be so wrong?

But who really knows if the crowd is headed in the right direction? Proverbs 16:25 says, "There is a way that appears to be right, but in the end it leads to death." Jesus said, "Enter through the narrow gate. For wide is the gate and broad is the road that leads to destruction, and many enter through it. But small is the gate and narrow the road that leads to life, and only a few find it" (Matthew 7:13,14).

So much of the pressure of performance comes from overvaluing what our peers are doing and believing that imitating them will make us somebody. For example, parents, sports clubs and art clubs do not set the agenda for your family. Their rules and demands may make you feel like you are doing the right thing because you see hundreds of other parents doing it. At the same time, the expectations of those groups can pile up on your shoulders until you are physically, mentally, and emotionally exhausted (on top of the countless other ways that you are burdened under the pressure of performance).

There may be nothing wrong with your participation in a few groups, programs, and events, but you need to make decisions about investing yourself and your family based upon what is right, what is God-pleasing, what is beneficial for everyone in the long run. It must not be based upon the fact that so many others have made this choice and it makes you feel like a good parent, spouse, employee, or citizen—like somebody—to do it. We hated it when our parents said, "If all your friends jumped off a cliff, would you too?" But then, many of us became parents and said the exact same thing—because we realized there was wisdom in it. Are we in danger of doing the very thing we warn our kids about?

This same performance pressure is often present in the church. We easily give each other the impression that *real* Christians do such and such: get up early and read the Bible at least an hour every day;

go on mission trips in Africa; attend multiple small groups; keep a spiritual journal, etc. If you don't do that, maybe you're not such a great Christian. But again, the question is not "What is the crowd doing?" or "What makes me feel like a somebody?" The question is "What is right, God-pleasing, and beneficial?"

The futility of a broken world

General Patton was known as a "git-er-done" kind of guy. During the middle years of World War II, he was trying to push the German army back in the Mediterranean theater, but his soldiers and equipment kept being siphoned off for a new major offensive planned for Normandy called Operation Overlord. This man of action was being crushed by the sense that he could not get done what he wanted to get done. On November 17, 1943, he wrote in his diary, "I have seldom passed a more miserable day. From commanding 240,000 men, I now have less than five thousand." On November 25, he wrote, "Thanksgiving Day. I had nothing to be thankful for, so I did not give thanks."[18] The danger of finding your somebody-ness through your performance is that sometimes, no matter how hard you try, things just don't get done.

It's a part of the curse that God warned Adam about after his fall into sin:

> To Adam [the LORD God] said, "Because you listened to your wife and ate fruit from the tree about which I commanded you, 'You must not eat from it,' cursed is the ground because of you; through painful toil you will eat food from it all the days of your life. It will produce thorns and thistles for you, and you will eat the plants of the field. By the sweat of your brow you will eat your food until you return to the ground, since from it you were taken; for dust you are and to dust you will return." (Genesis 3:17-19)

---

[18] Jeff Shaara, *The Rising Tide* (New York: Random House, 2006), Kindle file, Afterword.

Because sin has broken this beautiful world, even the grandest vision, the best-made plans, and perfectly executed tactics may still not accomplish what you hope. In fact, you might completely fail in what you set out to do, even as a child of God with the purest intentions.

Sometimes matters are simply beyond your control. You did all the research and then wisely invested thousands of dollars in a company that still went under. You spent hours praying for your relative and sharing the gospel, but in the end, she still refused to believe it. You planned to spend retirement traveling the globe, saving up your money and plotting out each itinerary, but cancer put an end to that. The world is broken. Things don't always turn out. James offers us sobering, godly wisdom for handling this:

> Now listen, you who say, "Today or tomorrow we will go to this or that city, spend a year there, carry on business and make money." Why, you do not even know what will happen tomorrow. What is your life? You are a mist that appears for a little while and then vanishes. Instead, you ought to say, "If it is the Lord's will, we will live and do this or that." (James 4:13-15)

Matt Perman wrote a fascinating book about productivity called *What's Best Next: How the Gospel Transforms the Way You Get Things Done*. I've never read another book that talks about productivity in light of the good news about Jesus, but this book does. And I love this disclaimer he offers near the end of the book:

> Though the things we talk about in this book *will* help make you more effective, I want to make it clear that I am not promising a "successful life" or any such thing. First, I see true success as a matter of serving others for God's glory, not as individual peace and affluence. But second, that reflects a sub-biblical view. The Bible does promise a measure of success—sometimes great success—to our wise and diligent efforts. "He who works his land will have plenty of bread" (Prov. 12:11). Our ordinary

expectation should be that if we work hard, work wise, and are generous, things will turn out well. But along the way, we will experience much hardship, difficulty, and even failure, because we live in a fallen world that is saturated with injustice. So the last thing I want anybody to come away from this book with is the notion that biblical productivity means a life of unending success, as we typically define it. Not true. Not true in the slightest. This is one of the great paradoxes of biblical effectiveness: often it doesn't produce any results; in fact, it seems to produce counterproductive results for at time.[19]

In other words, even if we work hard for all the right reasons, there is no guarantee of success, at least not the way we humans may define it. That doesn't mean you are doing something wrong; sometimes, that's just the way the world is.

Besides all this, you can't be a peak performer forever. You are getting older. You are older now than when you read the last sentence. And still older now. Older yet. Eventually, you will not be able to see this page as clearly as you did when you were 20. You will probably have put this book down a little more often to pee. You will not be able to finish all that you could finish in one day when you were 35. Ultimately, you are going to pass away. There is no working in the grave.

Perhaps you will have left some good work behind that will continue long after you are gone, like Apple soldiers on without Steve Jobs, but time is hard on everyone's work and memory. It doesn't take long for the memory of the deceased and their work to fade from the minds of the living. One of the most sobering things a friend ever said to me was "Cemeteries are filled with the bodies of people that no one could live without."

So the best we can do is to continue to work hard but rest well in the assurance that Jesus accomplished everything necessary to make

---

[19] Matt Perman, *What's Best Next* (Grand Rapids: Zondervan, 2014), Kindle file, Chapter 25.

us acceptable to God. This is the reason why the prophet Habbakuk could write these puzzling words:

> Though the fig tree does not bud and there are no grapes on the vines, though the olive crop fails and the fields produce no food, though there are no sheep in the pen and no cattle in the stalls, yet I will rejoice in the Lord, I will be joyful in God my Savior. The Sovereign Lord is my strength; he makes my feet like the feet of a deer, he enables me to tread on the heights. (Habakkuk 3:17-19)

Work hard; rest well. The sovereign Lord is your strength. He will carry you through both success and the lack of it.

Back to the young man on the stage. The father wasn't sure what to say at first, but then he asked his son to go back to the stage in his mind. He asked his sobbing child to imagine that Jesus was on that stage next to him. They were performing together in front of the entire crowd. While the young man took the wrong steps and messed up the choreography multiple times, Jesus would nail it every time. While the young man kept missing the notes, Jesus was pitch-perfect. At first, the young man was embarrassed and frustrated. He couldn't keep up with perfection. He always fell short. And then, as the noose came down to yank the young man violently offstage, Jesus masterfully grabbed the noose (without missing a single step) and put it around his own neck. He was violently ripped away, a man who never did anything wrong for a child who never seemed to get anything right.

The young man was left alone on the stage. The audience was still staring: some with disappointment, others with expectation. But suddenly, it didn't really matter what they thought anymore. The young man somehow knew that his partner had endured the fate of the failed performer so that this young man could continue to learn how to dance and sing without fear. He knew that the divine director was now somehow looking at him with expectation to see what kind of a performer he would become. He wasn't a judge; he was a proud parent.

The father then encouraged this young man to go back to those moments, some of them many years ago, when he had failed. The father encouraged his son to imagine the situation all over again, to imagine Jesus standing in his place. Just as the young man was failing, Jesus would step in and get it right. When the young man was just about to say the wrong words, Jesus said the right ones. When the young man was just about to hurt someone, Jesus showed that person kindness. And slowly, but surely, the young man began to learn how to dance and sing and serve and love.

Are you feeling the pressure of performance? Can you feel failure's noose tightening around your neck? Look to your Savior in perfect step with perfect pitch. Leave the past, the present, and the future in the capable hands of your successful Savior.

Superior Somebodies

You can boast about anything if it's all you have. Maybe the less you have, the more you are required to boast.

—John Steinbeck, *East of Eden*

Our huffing and puffing to impress God, our scrambling for brownie points, our thrashing about trying to fix ourselves while hiding our pettiness and wallowing in guilt are nauseating to God and are a flat denial of the gospel of grace.

—Brennan Manning,
The Ragamuffin Gospel

My new acquaintance, Michael, was plagued by some serious religious questions. In particular, he was wrestling with the idea that Christianity claims to be the only way to the true God. It didn't make any sense to him; it felt arrogant and divisive to make such a claim. His issue with Christianity is a common one, and it reminds me of a shirt I saw once. It displayed the symbols of Christianity, Buddhism, Judaism, and Islam in a long row together. Underneath them it said, "Too big for just one religion."

Michael explained his frustration to me in a very illustrative way. He asked me to imagine that there is an enormous mountain, and God is sitting at the summit. He passionately drew the picture for me: "Christians might go up the north side to get to God; maybe Muslims go up the south side; maybe Jews go up the west side; and Buddhists the east. They all take different paths to get to God, but they are all climbing up to God in the best way that they know how. How can Christians say their way is better?"

Over the years, I have found that illustration extremely useful. First of all, when religion is viewed as climbing up to God, you expect to find people at all different heights along the side of the mountain—most of them near the bottom, some at the middle, and a few, the truly devoted, somewhere near the top. You expect that some people will be trekking the clearly marked paths that wind up the side of the mountain, and others will go off-trail to make their own way. Furthermore, you expect to find a handful of special gurus at the summit, people like the Buddha, Gandhi, Jesus, and Mohammed, shouting directions down to the others: "Circle back around over there; use your hands to get past that slippery spot." This is the essence of natural religion: people figuring out the best way to make their way up to God with some help from the gurus.

Scrambling up the mountain

As you scramble up the mountain yourself, you naturally begin grading people on their progress. Who's above me on the mountain trek? Who's below me? And what's with those people who never seem to make it out of base camp? If they were more enlightened, they would know that they will never reach God by lounging around the lodge. They need to get moving. And what's with those people wandering back and forth in the foothills? They always have good intentions, but they never seem to make any headway—too little dedication. You have to be more committed, man. You need to meditate more like that guru at the summit or sacrifice a bit more like . . . well, like me. And speaking of that, I need to keep climbing. I will never catch up to the enlightened ones at this rate. I need more grit, more focus.

As you clamber up the rocks, you begin to feel a little superior to some hikers on the mountain. You discover that you have secretly been judging all those below you in subtle ways, ways that you probably wouldn't tell others because it might make you appear arrogant (farther down the mountain than you think you actually are)—but it's there.

This was the point of one of Jesus' parables:

> To some who were confident of their own righteousness and looked down on everyone else, Jesus told this parable: "Two men went up to the temple to pray, one a Pharisee and the other a tax collector. The Pharisee stood by himself and prayed: 'God, I thank you that I am not like other people—robbers, evildoers, adulterers—or even like this tax collector. I fast twice a week and give a tenth of all I get.'
>
> "But the tax collector stood at a distance. He would not even look up to heaven, but beat his breast and said, 'God, have mercy on me, a sinner.'
>
> "I tell you that this man, rather than the other, went home justified before God. For all those who exalt themselves will be humbled, and those who humble themselves will be exalted." (Luke 18:9-14)

The Pharisees were proficient hikers on Mount Religion. These are the men who had memorized the first five books of the Bible (yeah, including the long ones with all the regulations about animal sacrifices and kosher foods). These are the guys who followed over six hundred extra man-made mandates designed to keep them from breaking God's laws, like guardrails along the cliffs. In the opinion of most other pilgrims around them, they were leaping up sheer rock faces like mountain goats, and they were all nearing the summit. They were king of the hill in the church.

But notice all the comparing and judging in the Pharisee's prayer: "God, I thank you that I am not like other people—robbers, evildoers, adulterers—or even like this tax collector." Jesus gives us a glimpse of what really goes on at the heart of natural religion, whatever religion you adhere to—Buddhism, Hinduism, Islam, Christianity—whatever.

When we embrace natural religion, we are essentially attempting to become somebody by what we do as we scramble the mountain up to God. We are attempting to show that we can become acceptable to him and others. And that inevitably leads to the judgmental ranking of people on the mountain, just like the Pharisee did to the tax collector.

It happens to all of us, even those of us who profess that we are saved by grace alone, but it's often so subtle that we cannot detect it in ourselves. Religious people like to profess that "all sin is the same in God's sight," but they don't really believe it deep down. It's often hidden in that little phrase, "At least I . . ." "I may not be perfect, but at least I try; at least I go to church; at least I love my spouse and take my kids to their soccer games and give at the office." "I'm no saint, but at least I don't look down on people of a different color." "I'm not the most religious person in the world, but at least I'm not a hypocrite." Don't you see it now? "I may not be too high up the mountain, but at least I'm higher than that loser, bless her heart."[20] I justify myself by my hard work, especially in relation to others—as if a holy God would use any fallen human being as the standard of acceptance in his sight.

It's like the sentiment I heard once from a very spiritual man: "If we all just practiced what our different religions teach, the world would be a much better place." It sounds pious, doesn't it? But what's behind it? Isn't there a little bit of the sense that "if all the people would just follow their religion *like I am doing,* then the world would be a better place"? We often feel like we are working hard while others are lounging around; we are becoming somebody, and they are not. One of the reasons some of us like reading the news feed is that it makes us feel a little bit better about ourselves. And if you don't read the news feed, you feel superior to those of us who do. We cannot escape the constant comparisons.

In the end, when you don't embrace the assurance that you are somebody, you are always in proof mode, whether it is in the church, the workplace, or the classroom. I need to prove that I am good enough, that I am better than others. If I work hard enough, God will accept me. This is the way of natural religion, whatever the label,

---

[20] I learned that in the church you can insult anyone and still be godly so long as you add "bless her heart" to the end of the offending sentence. "She is such a horrible gossip, bless her heart."

wherever the origin. Meanwhile, we look down on others, we often cover up our failure, and we get frustrated with people who don't notice just how hard we are working. This leads to religion in the worst sense—a separation of all people into *us* and *them*. We are the good people; they are the bad people. We have God's favor and they do not. And all of that, in turn, leads to judgmentalism that manifests itself in the bloodstained coat of lovelessness, apathy, hatred, bigotry, and even violence in the name of religion.

Still more, when we try to climb up to God by our grit, we forget that every breath we take is a gift from him. He is the one who gives us our abilities and our vocations. If we are successful parents, plumbers, politicians, or pastors, it is all because of him—because of the way he designed our bodies and minds, because of the heart that he keeps beating every second of every day. When we look down on those who just can't seem to get it together, we forget that the vast majority of what we have become is determined by factors we have little to no control over. So much of our success is determined by where and when we were born, who our parents were, where we went to school, etc. Try growing up in Haiti and see how successful you are by American standards. If our lives have any sense of accomplishment at all, it has little to do with us. How foolish for us to look down upon another soul who seems to be farther down the side of the mountain.

In the end, some of us must be called from wickedness to Christ. The younger son in the parable of the prodigal son was clearly wicked, selfish, and lazy—a sex, drugs, and rock 'n' roll kind of guy. But I would venture that most of us must be called from religion to Christ, like the older brother in the same parable, the one who thought that his father owed him something for behaving so much better than his little brother.

Nobody loves company

Often, by God's grace, a good bout of failure cures us of thinking that we are much higher on Mount Religion (or Mount Acceptance or Mount Success) than we actually are, but now a new problem develops. We often tumble into fear and despair, scrambling for toe-holds as we slide down the mountain. When this happens, we are tempted to grab the arms and ankles of other people we pass on the way. If we can't climb the mountain as well as we hoped, perhaps we will feel better with some company a little farther down.

Scientists once performed a strange experiment that involved ten monkeys, a cage, a banana, a ladder, and a hose that sprayed ice-cold water. First, five monkeys were locked in a cage where a banana hung from the ceiling with a ladder placed right underneath it. Of course, one of the monkeys immediately tried to climb the ladder and get the banana; that's what monkeys do. However, as soon as it started to climb, a researcher would spray it with ice-cold water. In fact, he would spray the other four monkeys too. He did the same for the next monkey that tried to climb and so on, until all five monkeys had learned the lesson: Climbing the ladder equals ice-cold water for everyone, so no one climb the ladder, okay?

After this, the researchers replaced one of the monkeys with a new one. As anticipated, the new monkey spotted the banana and tried to climb the ladder. However, the other monkeys knew the drill, so they pulled it down and beat it up. The new guy learned: no ladder, no banana—period. He had no idea why. He didn't even need to be sprayed with ice-cold water. He was not climbing that ladder again.

A scary thing happened next. The researchers kept replacing old monkeys with new ones, and the same thing happened every time (the new guy learned not to climb the ladder), until all five original monkeys were replaced. In the end, none of the five new monkeys had been sprayed with ice-cold water, but not a single one tried to get the banana. And not a single one knew why either. "That's right, Frank, we didn't get the banana, and we're not letting you get it either. We don't know why. It's just the way we do things around here. Don't ask questions."

You've heard the expression "misery loves company." It's also true of nobodies who have begun to suspect that their attempts at somebody-ness are beginning to fail. Isaiah said that in times of uncertainty and distress, "people will oppress each other—man against man, neighbor against neighbor. The young will rise up against the old, the nobody against the honored" (Isaiah 3:5). Like the monkeys, they think, "If I can't have the banana, no one's getting it."

I think of Dan, a kid two years ahead of me in grade school. His classmates would often make fun of him for being fat. He was unpopular and didn't have many friends. I lost track of Dan after grade school until I was in college when I went to work for a construction company where Dan was also working. Only now, Dan was a pretty big dude. He had more experience than me, and he was accepted by the other members of the crew. He was finally in a position over someone else, namely, me. He loved to boss me around; he constantly made jokes at my expense. It was clear that, after years of feeling like a nobody, he was going to make someone else feel the same—maybe it would even make him feel more like a somebody again.

To be quite honest, I probably made fun of him along with other kids in grade school (maybe not to his face because he was older than me), and why? Because I felt like a nobody and thought I could become a somebody at someone else's expense. For being a nerd in grade school and high school, I sure made fun of a lot of people. Can't you just see the monkeys pulling each other down and beating each other up?

Thankfully, we're all adults now, and that doesn't happen anymore. I hear you snickering! Yes, you in the back row! We're just more subtle about it now.

I can think of a few ways that we still *monkey around* in this way. First, social media. None of us views the post of another person and leaves a comment like "fat" or "stupid" or "ugly." No one selects the angry face emoji when someone shares their personal accomplishments. We would be social outcasts.[21] But aren't we just a bit satisfied when one of our annoying connections makes a foolish comment

---

[21] Apparently, there is no sarcastic "could you please talk more about yourself" emoji. I confess that I have looked for it, and I am not proud of that. I also confess that I have really wanted to *like* a post so that I could instantly *unlike* it, which is what I wanted to do in the first place. Again, not proud of that. This is what I am talking about.

or takes a less than flattering picture? Don't we just love those videos and posts where people make total fools of themselves? Darwin Awards, anyone? Or the nearly irresistible clickbait with titles like "See Richard *crush* Senator So-and-so in two minutes flat!" "Watch as Mrs. So-and-so *puts* these lame protesters *in their place.*" We cheer quietly, not only because we agree with Richard's cause or don't agree with those lame protesters, but because it makes us feel better about ourselves to see our opponents get yanked down off the ladder. It makes us feel like more of a somebody when nobodies are stepped on. If I can't get the banana, no one's getting the banana.

Second, gossip. Of course, there's just plain old unfiltered gossip. "Did you hear what Kevin did?" But some of us church folk are a bit more subtle about it. We talk a little too freely about other peoples' problems because we're concerned. Or we bring their issues as a prayer request to our study group and then just happen to spill out the savory details so people better understand the situation. We share juicy gems about family members or coworkers under the guise of seeking advice or needing to vent. It's all gossip. It secretly makes us feel like more of a somebody when another nobody looks bad. This is why Proverbs 18:8 says, "The words of a gossip are like choice morsels; they go down to the inmost parts." Gossip just tastes so good to desperate nobodies as they try to drag others down the mountain.

The way out

What is the way out of the trap of trying to become somebody by our Rocky Mountain rankings? What is the way out of the trap of judgmentalism on the one hand and dragging people down on the other? The nobody tax collector in the story we read before knew what to do. He would not even look up to heaven. He had long given up the idea that he could climb Mount Religion. Instead, he beat his breast and uttered, "God have mercy on me, a sinner." In other words, "There is no way I will ever be able to climb up to you. You must come to me, or I am lost."

Those who picture Christianity as just another way up the mountain don't really understand what it's all about. Christianity says that

God realized we could never climb Mount Morality to reach him in his perfection, so he came down to us. Galatians 4:4,5 says, "When the set time had fully come, God sent his Son, born of a woman, born under the law, to redeem those under the law, that we might receive adoption to sonship." He descended the mountain in humility to live with us, obey God for us, and sacrifice himself instead of us so that through his resurrection we could be declared acceptable to God and raised up to live with him at the summit forever.

Christianity is not a system of steps you must take to earn God's acceptance. It's the history of what God has done for us through Jesus. Christianity is not a list of rules, but it is a list of all the ways that God actively loves us in Christ. You don't have to climb the mountain to find God; he already came down to be with us. And he still comes down to you in his Word, Baptism, and the Holy Supper to assure you by all five of your senses, "You are accepted. You are loved."[22]

Martin Luther once said, "The heart of religion lies in its personal pronouns." Isaiah 53 is an excellent example: "*He* was pierced for our transgressions, *he* was crushed for our iniquities; the punishment that brought us peace was on *him,* and by *his* wounds we are healed. We all, like sheep, have gone astray, each of us has turned to our own way; and the Lord has laid on *him* the iniquity of us all" (verses 5 and 6, emphasis mine). We didn't need to climb up to God; he came down to us and did everything for us. All natural religions say, "*You* must climb up to God. *You* must do this or that to get right with God." Jesus says, "*I* climbed down to you. *I* did it all in your place." Everything that needs to be done to make you acceptable to God was done by him—everything. You must be born sinless and live perfectly every day of your life to be right with God; Jesus did that in your place. You must pay eternal punishment for your failures to be right with God; Jesus did that too on the cross. You don't need to cling to your

---

[22] People often accuse Christianity of being exclusive, but it is actually more inclusive than any religious or philosophical system. All people are welcomed into the family of God, no matter how *good* or *bad* they may be and no matter where they seem to be located on the mountain. God longs for them to be his children; that's why he came down the mountain to save them.

accomplishment but to Christ's accomplishment. In fact, he did all of that for you long before you even considered how you could earn it or make it up to him.

This is what takes the burden of achievement off our shoulders. We don't have to earn God's acceptance. God gives it to us in Christ. Even though we are often arrogant and judgmental, worse than those people we generally look down on, he accepts us anyway. It changes our perspective on those around us. We don't see them below us—or even above us—on the mountain. We just give God thanks that he has mercy on all people, including us.

Interlude

Let not [your sin] discourage you. For if [God] . . . casts none out that come to Him, why should you fear? Our sins are many, but His mercies are more.

—John Newton

You will again have compassion on us; you will tread our sins underfoot and hurl all our iniquities into the depths of the sea.

—Micah 7:19

As long as you know you're nobody very special, you'll be a very decent sort of Horse, on the whole, and taking one thing with another.

—The Hermit to Bree,
The Horse and His Boy

Some of you might be old enough to remember the opening montage of ABC's classic television show *Wide World of Sports.* And if you remember that, you undoubtedly remember hearing the phrase "the agony of defeat." You can probably still see it in your mind's eye: the downhill skier careening off the right side of the ski jump, only to plummet down the hill like a floppy windmill. Every time I saw it, I cringed.

That skier was Vinko Bogataj. At that time, we all knew him; we just didn't know his name or anything about him. What we knew was that he was one of the most famous failures in the history of sports. And we had weekly reminders of just how badly he had failed. Jim Spence, former ABC Sports executive, said, "I felt that perhaps, maybe, we were being exploitive in showing that spill week after week after week and that maybe we oughta remove Vinko from the billboard." Imagine if all your failures were replayed on the TV screen every week for people all over the country to watch in vibrant color!

What do you do when you finally realize the depths of your sin, when the agony of your defeat just keeps playing over and over in your mind, or when, worse yet, it's right out there for everyone to see? When you have no question in your mind that you are a nobody and have lost all shreds of somebody-ness? In one sense, it's actually not a bad place to be—but only for a brief moment.

Serial killer Jeffrey Dahmer was a monster. After looking up his name on Wikipedia, I don't want to write down even a tenth of the horrible things he did. It gives me the chills just to think about it. However, just before Mr. Dahmer died, I remember hearing him read a personal statement after he had been convicted and sentenced at his trial. The local radio station played the full recording of it as people listened in disbelief.[23] I stood there dumbfounded as Mr. Dahmer quoted the apostle Paul, "Christ Jesus came into the world to save sinners—of whom I am the worst" (1 Timothy 1:15). He then professed his faith in Jesus as Savior and Lord. Not long after that, he was brutally beaten to death in prison.

At the time, I remember many people debating the sincerity of his confession. Could such a horrible man really repent? Did he really believe, or was he using Christ as a way to garner sympathy from people or even God himself? Did he actually believe that he could somehow earn his way into God's good graces by becoming a Christian after all he had done?

As hard as it is for us to hear, we need to realize that Mr. Dahmer had one advantage most of us will never have: there was no possibility of Mr. Dahmer ever thinking that somehow he could earn God's acceptance by his own righteousness, and there was almost no danger of him thinking that he was better than anyone else.

---

[23] I remember exactly where I was. It was the middle of the afternoon, and I was working on the manufacturing line at Scot Pump, trying to pay my way through seminary.

It's like the parable of the lost son (Luke 15:11-32). Both of the father's sons were spiritually lost, in a sense—the one got lost in a distant country; the other managed to get lost right at home. Both disdained their father. It was just more apparent to the younger brother that he desperately needed his father's mercy. It was that realization that led him back home. The older brother was still trapped in the slavery of thinking he was somebody because of all the good he had done. It was his pride that prevented him from partying with the rest of the family.

There's an advantage to knowing that you are a nobody by nature.

When we finally get to the place where we despair of our own righteousness, when we finally decide that we need to stop trying to be somebody, that just means we may be in a perfect place for God's gospel work in our lives. God can't work through somebodies, that is, through people who think they are somebody because of who they are or what they have done. So if you know you are a nobody by nature, you're in a good place.

But there is a warning here too. Once you recognize you're nobody by nature, there's the danger that you will think yourself beyond redemption. Once you are in that dark and lonely place, you need to get out. You can't stay there. God doesn't want you to stay there; God wants you to lay hold of his grace and walk into his love.

Consider the difference between Jesus' students, Peter and Judas. Judas betrayed Jesus and handed him over to the authorities for 30 pieces of silver. Peter denied knowing Jesus three times to save his own cowardly carcass. Their arrogant illusions of courage and success were both shattered in a single, fateful act. Yet Peter repented and was restored as one of Jesus' disciples while Judas went out and hanged himself. It wasn't that Peter was a good man at heart and Judas an evil monster—both were devastated by their failure. The difference was this: To Peter, Christ was bigger than his shame. To Judas, Christ was smaller than his shame. "God couldn't ever forgive a person like me" is the talk of an arrogant person who thinks that he knows better than God. "Even though Jesus says, 'Whoever comes to me, I will never turn away,' I already got this all figured out, and I am beyond salvation."

Martin Luther's friend Spalatin once committed a sin that he was certain could never be forgiven, and he refused to be comforted with the good news of Jesus. Luther wrote to him:

> To be sure, the devil has now plucked from your heart all the beautiful Christian sermons concerning the grace and mercy of God in Christ by which you used to teach, admonish, and comfort others with a cheerful spirit and a great, buoyant courage. Or it must surely be that heretofore you have been only a trifling sinner, conscious only of paltry and insignificant faults and frailties.... Therefore my faithful request and admonition is that you join our company and associate with us, who are real, great, and hard-boiled sinners. You must by no means make Christ to seem paltry and trifling to us, as though He could be our Helper only when we want to be rid from imaginary, nominal, and childish sins. No, no! That would not be good for us. He must rather be a Savior and Redeemer from real, great, grievous, and damnable transgressions and iniquities, yea, from the very greatest and most shocking sins; to be brief, from all sins added together in a grand total.[24]

As long as we cling to our shreds of self-righteousness, we will always wonder if we really are somebody. Only when we realize that we come to Christ empty-handed—or better yet, Christ comes to us—will we be in a place to fully embrace the splendor of God's salvation through Jesus and realize with true joy in our hearts just how deeply we are loved. We will be real sinners, and Christ will be our real Savior.

There is no need to fear when you go empty-handed to Jesus. I love Paul David Tripp's definition of the gospel in his book *Dangerous Calling:* "The gospel declares that there is nothing that could ever be uncovered about you and me that hasn't already been covered by

---

[24] http://lutherantheology.com/uploads/works/walther/LG/lecture-12.html

the grace of Jesus." That's the perfect message for somebody who is afraid of being a nobody if people find out who he or she really is.

Part 3

A Special Spot for Nobodies

Who is like the Lord our God, the One who sits enthroned on high, who stoops down to look on the heavens and the earth? He raises the poor from the dust and lifts the needy from the ash heap; he seats them with princes, with the princes of his people.

—Psalm 113:5-8

God's greatness is seen in his regard for the un-great.

—Tim Keller,
The Songs of Jesus, p. 294

Almost everybody knows something about Abraham, the father of faith. Many people know at least a little about his wife, Sarah, but few people know anything about Hagar, Abraham and Sarah's Egyptian slave. In one of their weaker moments, Abraham and his barren wife hatched a deplorable scheme to produce an heir for their family. They ordered Hagar to have sex with Abraham so that, when she became pregnant and gave birth, Sarah could steal the baby for herself. (This is a good reminder that the biblical heroes of faith were just as broken and in need of deliverance as we are.) Hagar had no rights or say in the matter. There were no social services to whom she could report, no one to advocate for her, and nowhere she could run. In that culture she was property: a heifer to be bought, sold, and bred without a second thought. Look up *nobody* in the dictionary and you would see her picture.

As sure as an old soap opera, Sarah grew jealous of this pregnant young woman and drove her out into the desert. Thankfully, God has a special place in his heart for nobodies. Genesis 16:7-10,13 says:

> The angel of the LORD found Hagar near a spring in the desert; it was the spring that is beside the road to Shur. And he said, "Hagar, slave of Sarai, where have you come from, and where are you going?"
> "I'm running away from my mistress Sarai," she answered.
> Then the angel of the LORD told her, "Go back to your mistress and submit to her." The angel added, "I will increase your descendants so much that they will be too numerous to count."
> [Hagar] gave this name to the LORD who spoke to her: "You are the God who sees me," for she said, "I have now seen the One who sees me."

The Bible covers a span of more than four thousand years. During that entire time, God only spoke directly to a handful of men and women. And most of them, like Abraham, only heard verbally from him a few times in their entire lives. Plus, this is the first time in the Bible that the "angel of the LORD"—Jesus before he came to the earth as a human—shows up. At this point in Genesis, we are already about two thousand years into recorded history, and this—THIS—is the first time Jesus appears to anybody! Jesus speaks to this woman in a culture where women were second-class citizens. Still more, Hagar is an Egyptian, not a part of God's chosen people. She is a slave. She is a victim of rape and a homeless, single mother. Yet God speaks directly to her twice (another time in Genesis 21)! This is the God who saw her when no one else did.

Does that same God see you? Does that same God love you, accept you, value you? We have been saying that he does, but how do we really know? Because God has a special place in his heart for nobodies.

The Greatest Nobody

Does it not lead us up hither: that the devotion of God to his creatures is perfect? that he does not think about himself but about them? that he wants nothing for himself, but finds his blessedness in the outgoing of blessedness.

—George MacDonald

Do you know what your name means? I can tell you about the names in my family. Christine means "little Christ" or "servant of Christ." Madeline is the French rendition of Magdalene, as in Mary Magdalene, one of Jesus' closest companions on this earth. It doesn't have any particular meaning that I am aware of—it's simply the name of the town that Mary was from. Samuel means "God listens" and is actually the same as Ishmael. Caleb means "brave" or "little dog." Do you know what your name means? It's kind of fun to research, isn't it?

Today, for the most part, we pick baby names that are unique or go well with our last name or sound good for yelling at them, like "Matthew Dennis!" Occasionally, we name a child after a parent, a grandparent, or an aunt or uncle. In ancient times, names were often picked to reflect a certain trait or to teach something. For example, God changed Abram's name to Abraham, "father of many," because many nations would come from him. God changed Jacob's name, "the trickster," to Israel, which means "wrestles with God," because he wrestled persistently with God in prayer. God told David to give his son the name Jedidiah, which means "loved by the Lord," but we know him better by the other name David gave him: Solomon, which means "peace," because Solomon would inaugurate a reign of peace. The prophet Isaiah's boy was named Maher-Shalal-Hash-Baz, which means "quick to the plunder, swift to the spoil." That name was meant to teach people about God's approaching judgment.

Each of the multiple names given to the Son of God, such as Immanuel and Lamb of God, also points to an important aspect of his character and work, but let's look more closely at his birth name: Jesus. What does that name mean for us?

Over the years, the name of Jesus has invoked many different responses. Some have hollered it out when pinching their thumb in a door. Others have spat it out in anger as they fought against Christians. Still others have sung it, prayed it, and proclaimed it with passion. My prayer is that you would speak it with a thrill of excitement because the name Jesus means real peace and hope for you.

This is how the birth of Jesus the Messiah came about: His mother Mary was pledged to be married to Joseph, but before they came together, she was found to be pregnant through the Holy Spirit. Because Joseph her husband was faithful to the law, and yet did not want to expose her to public disgrace, he had in mind to divorce her quietly.

But after he had considered this, an angel of the Lord appeared to him in a dream and said, "Joseph son of David, do not be afraid to take Mary home as your wife, because what is conceived in her is from the Holy Spirit. She will give birth to a son, and you are to give him the name Jesus, because he will save his people from their sins."

All this took place to fulfill what the Lord had said through the prophet: "The virgin will conceive and give birth to a son, and they will call him Immanuel" (which means "God with us").

When Joseph woke up, he did what the angel of the Lord had commanded him and took Mary home as his wife. But he did not consummate their marriage until she gave birth to a son. And he gave him the name Jesus. (Matthew 1:18-25)

A nobody name

Notice in the passage that Mary was "found" to be with child. She probably didn't reveal it on her own. I mean, how do you tell your fiancé that you're pregnant by an immaculate conception and that it's not your fault? "Oops, I'm pregnant!" It seemed obvious to Joseph that she had cheated on him; he knew he wasn't the father. Even though he couldn't believe this would ever happen, it had.

But Mary wasn't lying! This was the promised Messiah, the Son of God himself, conceived by the Holy Spirit. This was the desired of nations, the Savior promised four thousand years before, the Prophet the Jewish nation had been awaiting since Moses walked the earth. Through years of pain, toil, and affliction, God's people had longingly scanned the horizon for his advent. He was finally coming! And with all those ancient expectations exploding in his mind, I bet Joseph was anticipating some powerful Old Testament name. Or maybe he was expecting an original name, something as complicated as Maher-Shalal-Hash-Baz, to show just how unique the Savior would be. But the angel said in verse 21, "You are to give him the name Jesus."

Jesus? Jesus is just the Greek way of saying the Jewish name Joshua, like Juan in Spanish equals John in English. Joshua was such a common, ordinary name; probably six or seven villagers in the little town of Nazareth shared it. When Jesus' synagogue teacher called for Joshua, three kids might have raised their hands. There are several Joshuas mentioned in the Old Testament. There's even a Joshua in the genealogy of Jesus' ancestors in Luke 3. Still today, the third most common boy name in the United States in 2005 was Joshua. The Greek version of the name Jesus was pretty common too. There's a fellow mentioned in the letter to the Colossian church called Jesus and another in Acts called Bar-Jesus, or the "Son of Jesus." And Barabbas, the guy chosen to be set free instead of Jesus when Jesus was on trial before he was crucified, is also called Jesus Barabbas by strong tradition. The name Jesus is still common in Hispanic cultures.

Okay, so he had an ordinary name, but at least he had an extraordinary lineage, right? After all, he was a descendant of the great King David. Well, yes, but . . . four women are mentioned in his genealogy (Matthew 1): Tamar, Rahab, Bathsheba, and Ruth. Tamar tricked her father-in-law into sleeping with her; Rahab was a former prostitute (we'll come back to her later); Bathsheba cheated on her faithful husband; Ruth was a foreigner—a Moabite, to be specific—and the Moabites were godless people. But don't smirk too much, men. The male ancestors of Jesus were worse. Judah was the father-in-law who slept with Tamar, thinking she was a prostitute (I am not even gonna try to explain that one; you need to read about it yourself in Genesis 38). David was the king who seduced Bathsheba and then murdered her husband. Solomon jettisoned God's love for hundreds of wayward wives. Amon was a king so wicked that he ruled for only two years before he was assassinated. Ahaziah made it one year. Jehoiachin made it three months. These guys were the poster boys for wickedness. These are all the ancestors of Jesus—a whole lot of zeroes in the bunch. His humble name certainly fits his humble and colorful lineage.

Okay, so he has an ordinary name and a messy lineage, but his birth was extraordinary, right? Well, yes and no. He was born in a humble backwoods town, the son of a humble teenage peasant; his adoptive father was a humble carpenter. His mom gave birth to him in a barn, or according to early church tradition, a cave—cold, damp, and smelly. And he's wrapped in strips of cloth. That was the traditional way to bundle up babies at the time, but Mary and Joseph were in such dire straits that Mary needed to wrap him herself after giving birth. There's no nurse or midwife to be found. Then he's laid in a manger, but a *manger* is just a fancy way of saying a "feeding trough" where farm animals eat hay—definitely not showcased in the IKEA line of baby furniture. Countless Christmas cards show a content little Christ Child complete with a bright, glowing halo around his head like he's been plugged into an outlet. There was definitely no halo but probably some remnants of blood and bits of hay in his hair.[25] On Christmas night, millions of Christians sing, "But little Lord Jesus, no crying he makes." Do you really think so? He was cold and hungry and feeling the initial pains of a fallen world. He had plenty of reasons to cry. The only grand announcement of his coming was an amazing choir of angels seemingly wasted on a few grungy shepherds stuck on night shift. His humble name fit his humble circumstances.

Let's just pause and contemplate those humble circumstances a bit more. Whenever God showed up in the Old Testament, it was in stunning power and glory. At various times, he appeared in a pillar of fire, in clouds and smoke, and in a thunderstorm. It was always so terrifying that nobody wanted to go near him. When his glory descended on Mount Sinai, the Israelites asked Moses to speak to him on their behalf so they wouldn't die. Later, when Moses asked to see his glory, God said, "Okay, but only my backside." We don't even know what that means, except that it means God was telling him, "You can't see my full glory without being obliterated. Remember the end of *Raiders of the Lost Ark*? Yeah, that, but messier."

Now think of how far Jesus came from that power and glory. The almighty God in a donkey's trough. It's more than downsizing from 2,100 square feet to 700 square feet. It's more than Queen Elizabeth moving from Buckingham Palace to the local Super 8. It's more than staying in a tent instead of a motel when you are on vacation. It's even more than moving from a Midwest suburb to some African country to live in a mud hut as a missionary. In that humble birth, the infinite God became finite. The immortal became mortal. The gargantuan became tiny and insignificant. The uncontainable was contained in five or six pounds of frail flesh. The Almighty became weak. The infinitely rich became the marginalized poor.

At least his life was extraordinary, right? Not for the first 30 of his 33 years on this earth. Ninety percent of his life was lived in obscurity on a little dot on the map, a town like Oatman, Arizona—a really nice place, I'm sure, if you don't mind wild burros walking your streets,

---

[25] A "haylo," as my punny wife pointed out.

but not the first place you'd expect God to take up residence. Maybe God would show up in New York or Los Angeles but not Oatman.

Well, come on! Jesus must have at least had an amazing childhood, right? The apocryphal gospels (written a few hundred years after Jesus' life) contain fanciful tales about him molding clay sparrows and bringing them to life, dropping a dried fish into the water and making it swim again, and turning naughty kids into goats,[26] but it's quite possible that Jesus didn't do any miracles growing up. In fact, he was so ordinary that the first 12 years of his life are summed up in these words: "The child grew and became strong; he was filled with wisdom, and the grace of God was on him" (Luke 2:40). Sounds a little boring, to be honest. Then after one incident at the age of 12, we hear nothing until he turns 30! His humble name fit his humble childhood.

At 30, he begins to preach and claims to be God's Son. But he's so ordinary that those who know him can't believe it—even after seeing his miracles! While preaching in his hometown, the listeners say, "'Isn't this the carpenter's son? Isn't his mother's name Mary, and aren't his brothers James, Joseph, Simon and Judas? Aren't all his sisters with us? Where then did this man get all these things?' And they took offense at him" (Matthew 13:55-57). John tells us that even his brothers thought he was nuts. I mean, imagine if your brother claimed to be God. Do you think you would believe him? The kid who once laughed so hard that milk came out his nose, the kid who filled his diapers just like you. Jesus was their big brother; he was Joshua son of Joseph, nothing more.[27] It's no wonder Isaiah prophesied seven hundred years before the birth of Jesus that he would have "no beauty or majesty to attract us to him, nothing in his appearance that we should desire him" (Isaiah 53:2). In a certain sense, he was as ordinary as his ordinary name.

---

[26] I really wish I could have done that when I was growing up.

[27] By the way, these facts make a strong case for the validity of the Bible. Do you think that if Jesus' followers were making up stories and trying to convince people that Jesus was God and Messiah, they would tell stories like this?

What does that mean for us in the present? There have been oodles of kids named Joshua raised in humble circumstances and little towns. Many kids are born to unwed mothers and adopted by fathers. Well, first of all, it convicts me. It's back to that trying-to-become-somebody-through-acceptance thing again. I have a natural propensity to want to see my name in lights! Nothing suits me better than to get a compliment: "Attaboy, Matt!" Or to have my name announced for all to hear over the loudspeaker: "Let me tell you what Matt did!" I want my voice to be heard: "Good idea, Matt!" I've even found myself fishing for compliments on projects: "Oh, I didn't do very good . . ." "Yes, you did, Matt!" And if I don't get heard or don't get my way, I have a right to lash out. After all, my name's on the line. We're big on our own names. So it's kind of convicting that when God comes to earth, he should choose such an ordinary name and ordinary circumstances while we work for notice and acclaim.

Second, the ordinary name of Jesus encourages us. The God who moves the Milky Way and hurtles Halley's Comet through the stars has hands just like yours. The Prince who plays with planets has a belly button in the same spot as yours. He got hungry, thirsty, tired, frustrated, sad, and hurt just like you. If you've felt it, so has he. The King of the universe is your brother, and he's proud of it!

The name Jesus/Joshua is also significant because it means "the Lord Jehovah saves." Jesus is the Lord Jehovah who doesn't sit on his hands. He acts; he saves. To him, love isn't a mushy feeling you fall into like tripping helplessly into a hidden pothole. It is action! He doesn't wait for you to come to him; he comes to you. He doesn't wait for you to earn his love or clean yourself up; he comes to you, to do right what you've done wrong and save you.

The One with other names like Wonderful Counselor, Mighty God, the great I AM, and the King of kings entered the world bloody and helpless as Jesus, son of Joseph, and left it in the same way. His first blood was shed in the cutting of that knotty cord that held him to his mother for sustenance. The last blood he shed would be mixed with his own sweat as it ran down the cross of his execution. In between those two days would be frustration, rejection, struggle, suffering, and pain. The one who had it all would be left with nothing in the end as he suffered the agony of hell for our guilt.

The movie *Saving Private Ryan* takes place during World War II. At the beginning of the movie, General George Marshall receives word that three of the four drafted sons of the Ryan family have been killed in battle. Determined not leave their mother childless, he dispatches Captain John Miller and a small team of soldiers to find the fourth son, Private James Ryan, a paratrooper who is missing in action somewhere in Normandy. Captain Miller and his team scour France to find Ryan as the war rages ruthlessly around them. In the end, Miller and all his men die with the exception of one, a platoon of good men sacrificed to save one—a man they don't even know.

Captain Miller was willing to do whatever it took to save Private Ryan, no matter the cost to himself, because it was his duty—but Jesus goes far beyond that! He *had* to move heaven and earth on that first Christmas; he *had* to humble himself. He *had* to do whatever it would take—and not because it was duty! It was his desire. Jesus so badly wanted you to know peace, purpose, and the wonders of heaven that he set forth that first Christmas into a cold and heartless world, leaving heaven far behind and taking on the ordinary name we have come to love so much.

A Nobody
for Everybody

I have not come to call the righteous, but sinners to repentance.

—Luke 5:32

I never knew how bad a heart I had. . . . Often I am tempted to think that one so full of sin cannot be a child of God at all. But I try to throw it back, and rejoice all the more in the preciousness of Jesus, and in the riches of that grace that has made us "accepted in the Beloved."

—Hudson Taylor, missionary to China

Are you humble enough to listen to a nobody? I wasn't. During my seminary years, my best friend and I were sitting in a booth at a fast-food restaurant, eating the fine cuisine that seminary students can actually afford. I was so proud of how much I was learning in school. I was under that dangerous spell so common for young theologians, thinking that my spiritual knowledge was equal to spiritual maturity and made me a qualified judge of everything. So I was expounding on how foolish another group of Christians was and why my way was so much better.

Suddenly, there stood up in the booth behind us one of the ugliest women I have ever seen in my life. Her hair looked like the nest of an old crow, filled with tangles and stray bits of straw (I may have imagined the straw, but that is how I still picture her decades later). Her wrinkled face was hideous; her eyes were watery and sickly. And hanging between her nostrils and her top lip was a web of gooey snot.

She gathered herself and said to us, "I like to think that, when I am talking, it is like I am speaking into a microphone and everyone is able to hear me. That way, I am more careful about what I say." I think I mumbled something about being sorry and then went back to conversing with my friend—albeit a little quieter than before.

To this day, I suspect that this woman was actually an angel in disguise. And I still regret that I didn't really listen to her at the time. I just thought she was some pathetic vagrant; and who was she to chastise me, a fairly successful, middle-class seminary student? It's hard to listen to someone we think is a nobody—especially when we think we are somebody.

So let's humble ourselves and listen to the criminal on the cross next to Jesus, someone who teaches us three key truths that every human must understand or be lost, three truths that some of the world's smartest people have never really understood or believed. First, see if you can spot the three truths:

> Two other men, both criminals, were also led out with him to be executed. When they came to the place called the Skull, they crucified him there, along with the criminals—one on his right, the other on his left. Jesus said, "Father, forgive them, for they do not know what they are doing." And they divided up his clothes by casting lots.
>
> The people stood watching, and the rulers even sneered at him. They said, "He saved others; let him save himself if he is God's Messiah, the Chosen One."
>
> The soldiers also came up and mocked him. They offered him wine vinegar and said, "If you are the king of the Jews, save yourself."
>
> There was a written notice above him, which read: THIS IS THE KING OF THE JEWS.
>
> One of the criminals who hung there hurled insults at him: "Aren't you the Messiah? Save yourself and us!"

But the other criminal rebuked him. "Don't you fear God," he said, "since you are under the same sentence? We are punished justly, for we are getting what our deeds deserve. But this man has done nothing wrong."
Then he said, "Jesus, remember me when you come into your kingdom."
Jesus answered him, "Truly I tell you, today you will be with me in paradise." (Luke 23:32-43)

Nobody's perfect

The criminal on the cross next to Jesus was an absolute wastrel. However, as we read the account of his final, agonizing moments on this earth, we sometimes clean him up a bit and ignore the depths of his depravity. We think that one of the criminals was evil and mocked Jesus, but the other one repented and trusted in him. The problem is that our minds trick us into thinking that one of those criminals was at least a little bit better than the other. He defended Jesus and was a pretty good guy with a bad rap; that's why he repented and believed.

But nothing could be further from the truth. Traditionally, he is called the thief on the cross, but in reality, *criminal* or *rebel* is a more appropriate term. The Roman authorities did not generally hang people on crosses for stealing a few bent shekels. He was most likely a rapist, a violent insurrectionist, or a murderer—maybe all three. And he was so wicked that he continued to hate even as he was hurtling toward hell. Mark 15:32 says, "Those crucified with [Jesus] also heaped insults on him." I remember when Timothy McVeigh was about to be executed after he was convicted of the 1995 Oklahoma City bombing that killed 168 innocent people, including 19 children in a day care center—there wasn't a single shred of remorse in his eyes or his words. Now picture this criminal hanging on the cross next to Jesus. Even in his excruciating pain, he was mocking Jesus to get a few laughs from his own executioners. It would be like two men on a plane that is going down. The one looks at the other and quips, "Ha, ha. You're going to die." They are on the same plane; they're both going to die!

Now would be a good time to make your peace with God, not make fun of the man next to you, but this criminal didn't care—at least not at first. So don't romanticize him.

By God's grace, he eventually came to his senses. Maybe it was what he had heard about Jesus before. Maybe it was the astonishing prayer Jesus offered even as the soldiers nailed him to the cross and the religious leaders mocked him: "Father, forgive them, for they do not know what they are doing." Maybe it was the reality that death was running him down like a screaming Black Rider, and he would soon have to account for his rebellion before a holy God. Most likely, it was a combination of all three. Whatever the reason, this nobody spoke the first key truth that we must understand or be lost: "Don't you fear God since you are under the same sentence? We are punished justly, for we are getting what our deeds deserve." This nobody criminal finally realized the terrifying reality: He was getting what he deserved, and this agony on the cross was merely the initial pinprick of the eternal destruction that awaited him.

Hopefully by now in this book you are not still clinging to any scraps of your own self-righteousness, your failed attempts to become somebody. But because I know how easily we fall back into these same sinful patterns, let me remind you—we must humbly and regularly accept the truth that this miserable man shared: We *should* be punished; we *should* get what our deeds deserve. Many people like to say, "Nobody's perfect." Sometimes it's said in a harmless way, like when we forget one of the digits of our Social Security number. Other times, it's said to trivialize our sin. "It's not that big of a deal. Besides, nobody's perfect." I am afraid that when it comes to the sin of trying to become somebody through who we are or what we do, we might be tempted to trivialize it. "So I try a little too hard to be liked. I'm just friendly." "So I work a little too hard. Sue me!" "So I like my cars and my home and my status a little too much. What's the real harm?" It *is* a big deal! Trying to become somebody with our selfish methods for our own selfish ends has consequences. How many generations are affected negatively by the abuse of someone who desperately tried to become somebody only to burn out and turn to self-medication through alcohol or marital infidelity? I have counseled people whose lives have been shattered by the abuse of others and find themselves pulled into the same unhealthy patterns. How many neglected children turn into negligent parents? How many children of workaholics surpass their parents and make life even harder on their kids than it was for them? How many abused children have been devastated by the silence of one who was too cowardly to speak up on their behalf?

Our lame attempts at somebody-ness have painful consequences for us and others. That's sin. With the criminal we need to recognize that we should be getting what our sins deserve. It's true that nobody's perfect. And it's a reason we all desperately need a Savior.

The perfect nobody

The hateful, hard-hearted criminal next to Jesus also realized this: "No matter how much mud we fling at this guy, he doesn't fling it back! In fact, he asks God to forgive us." Clearly, this man wasn't your ordinary criminal, not like the perverts he had met in prison or the swindlers he had swapped stories with. So he spoke the second truth that we must understand or be lost: "This man has done nothing wrong." A lot of prisoners on death row insist that they are innocent; that doesn't make it so any more than saying, "I am a cheeseburger," makes you a Whopper. But this hardened criminal realized that he was witnessing a gross miscarriage of justice. Jesus didn't belong on that cross!

He probably didn't understand the fullness of that discovery at the time. Jesus was not only innocent of execution-deserving crimes, but he was innocent of all guilt. In his 33 years of existence, he had never sinned once in word, deed, or thought. In fact, Jesus once asked his enemies if any of them could accuse him of wrong (John 8:46). As much as they hated him, not one of them was foolish enough to dispute that point. Not only did this *criminal* not belong on a cross, this King of the Jews belonged on a throne—justly judging the criminals, the executioners, the gawking crowd, the whole world.

This is what theologians call the active obedience of Christ, and it is essential for our salvation. We Christians spend a lot of time talking about Jesus' death on the cross, but his death wouldn't have any real significance without his perfect life. In order to be accepted by God and spend eternity in his perfect presence, we not only need to be forgiven (that is a negative need), but we also need to be innocent (that is a positive need). We not only need to be free of guilt, but we also need to be full of good. So Jesus not only had to die the death we would have, but he had to live the life we should have. And that's just what he did. The missionary Paul explained it this way: "God made him who had no sin to be sin for us, so that in him we might become the righteousness of God" (2 Corinthians 5:21). Since we have sin, Jesus became sin for us on the cross. In order for God to be just, he must punish sin, so Jesus volunteered to take the punishment. That's what theologians call the passive obedience of Christ. But don't miss the other part: The One who had no sin became sin for us so that we might become "the righteousness of God." How can criminals like us possibly become good enough to be accepted by God? We must have the righteousness of Christ.

Thus, during that dreadful moment on Calvary, a great exchange was being transacted in the eyes of heaven: Christ becoming criminal and the criminal becoming clean. Even while the noxious shame of his wasted existence filled the nostrils of those who watched, the sinner became a saint. The cross at the center was now the temporal residence of a man justly condemned to die, a man who had never done anything wrong.

Kids often say: "Not fair! She got two scoops of ice cream and I only got one." "Not fair! He got 30 minutes on the iPad, and I only got 10!" But this great exchange at the cross really is not fair! It's not fair that the perfect Son of God would be condemned to writhe like a worm on a fishhook while the embodiment of worthlessness goes to heaven after doing nothing good! And yet that is the message of undeserved love for all who are humble enough to kneel at the foot of the cross and cry out, "Mercy!"

The nobody for everybody

But is this true for somebody like me? If pride is at one end of the spectrum of trying to become somebody before God, despair is at the other. Despair is, in fact, one of the worst sins, not because it is so much worse than all the others but because it threatens to close us off from the only one who can offer us real hope and peace. So learn this third truth from the criminal: No matter who you are, how badly you have sinned, or how defiled you feel, there is true hope in Jesus, because Jesus is the Nobody for everybody.

As this dying criminal realized that the man next to him was no criminal, he may have thought back to those stories he had learned as a boy. They say that some of your last thoughts in this life come from your earliest memories. Maybe he remembered learning how God had promised that one of Abraham's descendants would bless all the nations. Maybe he remembered what his parents had taught him about the King who would rise up from the rotting stump of King David's family tree to establish his eternal kingdom and rule forever. Maybe he remembered what he had learned about the great Suffering Servant who would be a blood offering for our sin, who would again see the light of life and be satisfied, and who would rule throughout all generations. Maybe he remembered hearing Psalm 22 read in synagogue school and realized it perfectly described the man hanging next to him on the cross:

> My mouth is dried up like a potsherd, and my tongue sticks to the roof of my mouth; you lay me in the dust of death. Dogs surround me, a pack of villains encircles me; they pierce my hands and my feet. All my bones are on display; people stare and gloat over me. They divide my clothes among them and cast lots for my garment. (verses 15-18)

As he grew up and experienced the real world, he had dismissed all these prophecies as fairy tales, the wild fantasies of a people oppressed. But it all began to come back to him now.

Still more, he had undoubtedly heard rumors of this Jesus, now naked and broken beside him. The man who ate with prostitutes and tax collectors. The man who touched defiled lepers and cleansed them. The man who made the blind see, the deaf hear, and the dead rise. Maybe he had even heard snatches of Jesus' teaching: "Come to me, all you who are weary and burdened, and I will give you rest." "I am the bread of life. Whoever comes to me will never go hungry, and whoever believes in me will never be thirsty." "Let anyone who is thirsty come to me and drink. Whoever believes in me, as Scripture has said, rivers of living water will flow from within them." "For even the Son of Man did not come to be served, but to serve, and to give his life as a ransom for many." Could he be the one? And would he really welcome even someone like me? Jesus did say, "*All you* who are weary and burdened." He did say, "*Whoever* believes in me." That was enough for this broken loser. Convinced that Jesus was the long-expected Messiah, the criminal pleaded, "Jesus, remember me when you come into your kingdom."

Jesus immediately responded, "Truly I tell you, today you will be with me in paradise." It's such a beautiful little word: *will*. Notice that he didn't say, "You wasted your entire life and now you come running to me at the 11th hour?" Or even, "Today you *might* be with me in paradise, if you really turn your life around, following these five simple steps." No: "Today you *will* be with me in paradise." Wow! This vile criminal, the chief of sinners, was saved even as death's sickle was descending. He was saved from God's wrath by God himself, who was dying on the cross beside him.

And notice what else Jesus told him: "You will be *with me*." Not, "I have a few extra tickets up in the nosebleed seats if you still want to come to my concert. I am sure we can squeeze you in." Nope. "You will be *with me*." Front row seats and backstage passes! Jesus has a million matters on his mind and a billion sins on his soul, but all he can think about in that moment is this hopeless, tormented soul beside him, as if that criminal had always been his best friend and faithful companion. Jesus was looking forward to spending eternity with this precious child.

And finally notice: "You will be with me *in paradise*." The criminal was probably hoping for crumbs, and Jesus offered him an eternal banquet, like the heavenly feast Isaiah had described over seven hundred years before.

On this mountain the Lord Almighty will prepare a feast of rich food for all peoples, a banquet of aged wine—the best of meats and the finest of wines. On this mountain he will destroy the shroud that enfolds all peoples, the sheet that covers all nations; he will swallow up death forever. The Sovereign Lord will wipe away the tears from all faces; he will remove his people's disgrace from all the earth. The Lord has spoken. (Isaiah 25:6-8)

Think of what that banquet meant to a man dying of dehydration as he lost excessive amounts of blood and other bodily fluids, to a man who had eaten nothing but the hard bread of bitterness. Jesus would swallow up death and make this excruciating pain seem like a distant dream and then no more. Jesus would wipe away every tear of regret for the lives this man had ruined. Jesus would remove the disgrace of being an embarrassment to his family. This parched man, barely able to speak, would shout out Jesus' praises forever in heaven. Just a few more minutes to wait, and all would be well. Better than well—all would be paradise.

What did he do to be invited into that banquet? Nothing. What had he done to show that he didn't deserve it? Everything. Yet Jesus gladly took him in. And Jesus takes you in too.

The Resurrection for Nobodies

[The witch] would have known that when a willing victim who had committed no treachery was killed in a traitor's stead, the Table would crack and Death itself would start working backward.

—C. S. Lewis,
*The Lion, the Witch and
the Wardrobe*

A few days after Christine and I got married, we packed our meager belongings in a U-Haul and headed to Columbia, Tennessee, for my seminary internship year. Christine was called by my intern congregation to be the director of their new preschool. It was an exciting adventure for us, a honeymoon year on our own to discover the ups and downs of life together.

Shortly after arriving in our new hometown, Christine attended a local seminar about transitions. The facilitator gave the attendees an impromptu test to rate their stress level. "If you have just gotten married, add 50 points." Check. "If you have just moved to a new city, add 50 points." Check. "If you have just started a new career, add 50 points." Check. "If your significant other has just started a new career, add 50 points." Check. Christine was on her way to scoring 500 points on a scale of 400.

So we did what we could to soften the transition . . . we got a puppy! If that had been on the test, the facilitator would have probably said, "If you have recently been through eight transitions already and decided to get a dog, add 300 points and check yourself into the psych ward at your local hospital. Or else, curl up right here into the fetal position and have a good cry."

It was a kind of experiment. Christine told our friends that if we didn't mess up the dog, maybe we wouldn't mess up our children, if and when God blessed us with them. It did not bode well for our children. We had no idea what we were doing.

Around the same time, we took a shot at raising plants. Well, there was just one plant, and his name was Herman.

I don't know why we named the plant Herman. We didn't take a lot of time to pick just the right name; we didn't pick it because of some particular quality about him. He was just Herman.[28] And don't ask me what kind of plant he was; he was green and had broad leaves but longer than they were broad. As I look back, I feel bad about poor Herman. We neglected him, plain and simple. We would go for weeks without watering him. We would position him in corners that had less sunlight than Carlsbad Caverns and yet expect him to flourish. As a result, Herman would sadly wilt, his broad leaves drooping over the edge of his pot like sickly, lime-colored bed sheets. After weeks, we would finally notice his sorry state. Then we would water him and move him to a sunnier spot, hoping beyond hope that he would recover.

And he did—so many times, in fact, that we started to think it was miraculous. A few days after watering, he would be return to his former, cheery self, unaware that another round of neglect was soon on its way.

He went on like this for months, until one day, he truly died. No flood of water, no mighty dose of sun would bring him back. After weeks of failed plant CPR, we threw him away. Poor Herman.

Here's a reality that's often difficult to contemplate (maybe even to believe) in a culture obsessed with youth, beauty, and health: Whether you treat your body like Herman or not, it's gonna end up like Herman someday—dead. Taking thousands of multivitamins, following

---

[28] Okay, Christine just told me why. She wanted to name him Herman after her college roommate whose last name was Herman—a woman who was the picture of die-hard power.

fabulous fitness plans, eating organic food and using organic soap (maybe), getting plenty of sleep, reducing your stress—these may all stave off the grim reaper for a while, but you're still going to die.

Thanks for the encouraging message! *I'm gonna close your book now and eat a whole bag of Cheetos while reading something more cheery, like *Angela's Ashes*.*

Oh, but I'm not finished: You are also going to rise again—because Jesus did.

The resurrection of Jesus changes everything

Saturday must have been miserable for the small band of Jesus' followers who had not immediately disbanded after his dishonorable death on Friday. They had seen a lot of things—Jesus healing the blind and the lame, casting out demons, and even raising people from the dead—but didn't you see how broken he was on that cross? Nobody comes back from something like that. Besides, they had thought he was riding into Jerusalem to reign, not to be ripped apart and nailed up like the pelt of a desecrated animal. So many dreams dashed in just a few horrific hours. Saturday was a day of rest, but there was no rest for this small group of leaderless misfits.

When Sunday morning finally wheezed in, nothing had changed, except that a bit more reality had set in: They were finished. It was time to get back to real life, to get back to what they should have been doing in the first place instead of chasing a rabbi around the country. Some women in their group headed to Jesus' tomb to finish the proper preparations for his burial and get some closure. I mean, what else did they really have to do? "After the Sabbath, at dawn on the first day of the week, Mary Magdalene and the other Mary went to look at the tomb" (Matthew 28:1).

They went expecting nothing; nothing changes much in a cemetery. Occasionally a new body is brought in. Sometimes people remove the old plastic flowers to add new ones, but cemeteries are known for their silent and consistent message, "This is where you will be someday too—unmoving, unchanging—forever." Not even the miracle worker could change that fate—everybody's fate.

There was a violent earthquake, for an angel of the Lord came down from heaven and, going to the tomb, rolled back the stone and sat on it. His appearance was like lightning, and his clothes were white as snow. The guards were so afraid of him that they shook and became like dead men.

The angel said to the women, "Do not be afraid, for I know that you are looking for Jesus, who was crucified. He is not here; he has risen, just as he said. Come and see the place where he lay. Then go quickly and tell his disciples: 'He has risen from the dead and is going ahead of you into Galilee. There you will see him.' Now I have told you."

So the women hurried away from the tomb, afraid yet filled with joy, and ran to tell his disciples. Suddenly Jesus met them. "Greetings," he said. They came to him, clasped his feet and worshiped him. Then Jesus said to them, "Do not be afraid. Go and tell my brothers to go to Galilee; there they will see me." (Matthew 28:2-10)

On this particular morning, the deathly silence of the graveyard was drowned out by the thunderous rumble of an earthquake, the ponderous grind of stone on stone, the raucous clatter of weapons and armored bodies hitting the ground, followed by the booming voice of God's messenger: "Do not be afraid, for I know that you are looking for Jesus, who was crucified. He is not here; he has risen, just as he said."

It reminds me of the time our family went to see the movie rendition of *The Lion, the Witch and the Wardrobe*. We were in a large, packed theater. In fact, we arrived too late and had to sit in the very last row. There is a moving scene in the movie just after the great lion Aslan, a symbol of Jesus Christ, has sacrificed his life to save the traitor Edmund. Aslan's desecrated, lifeless body lays limp on the Stone Table where he has been sacrificed. The theater was cemetery silent. Every person felt the emotional weight of that moment

. . . when suddenly, my son Caleb, who was probably 4 at the time, yelled out at the top of his lungs from the very last row, "Oh, yeah! But he's comin' back!" Moments later, the Stone Table cracked, and Aslan rose from the dead.

As the earth shook, the stone rolled, and the angel spoke; everything in the universe shouted out, "Oh, yeah! But he's comin' back!"

Just like dead Herman, you can't bring dead people back to life. There is no magic potion or miracle drug that can reinsert the soul, reboot a cold brain, and reconfigure millions of rotting cells to resuscitate the deceased. Scientists, magicians, and preachers have been trying and failing since before history recorded it. And when Jesus' body lay in that tomb, he was completely gone; there was nothing left but the shell that had once been a person.

And yet God the Father raised him up. He reinserted the soul; he rebooted the brain; he reinvigorated his lifeless body so that life came rushing back in. Dead people don't walk, but this one did—shattering the grim constancy of the cemetery. Suddenly, everything changed—forever!

What exactly changed? First of all, you got proof. In the last chapter, we noted that Jesus had to live a perfect life and die a hellish death in our place. But a lot of prophets have died gruesome deaths, and none of them have come back. What makes this death different? How are we supposed to know that this innocent life and death count for anything? The great missionary Paul once wrote:

> [Jesus] was delivered over to death for our sins and was raised to life for our justification. Therefore, since we have been justified through faith, we have peace with God through our Lord Jesus Christ, through whom we have gained access by faith into this grace in which we now stand. And we boast in the hope of the glory of God. (Romans 4:25–5:2)

He literally says, "Jesus was delivered over to death *because of* our sins and was raised to life *because of* our justification." *Justification* is just a fancy Bible word that means "to declare someone innocent."

In other words, Jesus' resurrection is proof that you are innocent and acceptable to a holy God. In his sight, you are perfect! You will never be judged or accepted on your performance but upon the performance of the resurrected Christ.

It is critical for you to understand this truth. You are not just forgiven. It's not like God begrudgingly said, "Fine, I will not be angry at him anymore." Let me say it again: You are justified, declared innocent before God, as one beloved coworker once taught me, "just as if I'd never sinned." You don't have to do *anything* to make yourself acceptable to God. When God looks at you through faith in Jesus, he sees the perfect life of Jesus given as a gift to you, and he is pleased. He says, "Well done, good and faithful servant," and he invites you into his presence.

This is the whole reason the prophet Zephaniah could write these astonishing words to people who had failed God countless times: "The LORD your God is with you, the Mighty Warrior who saves. He will take great delight in you; in his love he will no longer rebuke you, but will rejoice over you with singing" (3:17). God delights in you because he delights in Jesus who lived a perfect life in your place, died as punishment for your guilt, and rose to guarantee that you are now innocent in God's sight. When God looks at you, he sees a billion reasons to rejoice and sing.

Some people desperately wish they could start over and put their shameful past behind them forever. Through the resurrection you can. It's all gone, all forgiven, all erased—past, present, and future. In fact, if there had been just one sin left to your account, one tiny misstep that Christ had missed, his body would still be lying in a tomb somewhere in Israel today. But Christ has indeed been raised, the guarantee that your status has changed!

Second, your capability changed. You are not a poor, helpless nobody anymore. Through the resurrection of Jesus, sin and Satan no longer have any power over you. They no longer have the power to strangle you with guilt and cripple you with shame. You need not obey their voice any longer. Paul says:

We were therefore buried with him through baptism into death in order that, just as Christ was raised from the dead through the glory of the Father, we too may live a new life. For if we have been united with him in a death like his, we will certainly also be united with him in a resurrection like his. For we know that our old self was crucified with him so that the body ruled by sin might be done away with, that we should no longer be slaves to sin—because anyone who has died has been set free from sin. (Romans 6:4-7)

You aren't a victim of your destructive patterns anymore. You are not shackled to the hopeless cycle of desperately seeking somebody-ness. You are not a victim of your past, your failures, your upbringing, or what was done to you. That old nobody was buried with Christ, but the new somebody was raised up with him to live a brand-new life, free from the icy talons of sin and Satan.

A World War II veteran once told me that when he was in the Philippines clearing out a 40-acre plot for their new PT boat base, he came across a snake. This wasn't any snake; this was a 20-foot monster, about 8 inches in diameter. This wasn't a snake you let wander around a camp full of people. So this vet got out the forklift, drove it out to the field, and ran that snake over—and that was the end of the snake. It still looked terrifying; all the men went out to marvel at its size, but there wasn't anything to be afraid of anymore. The forklift had seen to that. Jesus crushed the heads of sin and Satan, those venomous snakes, when he took that first momentous step out of the tomb. Sin and Satan still try to scare us, but Jesus ran them over for good. They've lost their power over you.

And finally, the resurrection changes your future. Paul puts it this way:

I pray that the eyes of your heart may be enlightened in order that you may know the hope to which he has called you, the riches of his glorious inheritance in his holy people, and his incomparably great power for us who believe. That power is the same as the mighty strength he exerted when he raised Christ from the dead and seated him at his right hand in the heavenly realms, far above all rule and authority, power and dominion, and every name that is invoked, not only in the present age but also in the one to come. And God placed all things under his feet and appointed him to be head over everything for the church, which is his body, the fullness of him who fills everything in every way. (Ephesians 1:18-23)

First, Jesus' resurrection changes your *immediate* future. When God raised Jesus from the dead, he exalted him to the highest throne of authority in the heavenly realms. Everything and everyone are in submission to him at all times. Jesus isn't a wandering, penniless peasant anymore, but our victorious Savior, the King of kings and Lord of lords, who fills the whole universe and works out all things for the good of the church both now and forever. Even knowing Jesus and his glorious salvation, there will still be times you feel like an absolute nobody: when the weight of the world threatens to crush your hopes; when people treat you like trash; when you carry the burden of brokenness around in your body through weakness, anxiety, or disease. But remember, Jesus is risen and rules over the entire universe for your good. He will pull you through all this for his glory and your good! Your future on this earth is guaranteed to have his blessing.

Second, Jesus' resurrection also changes your *eternal* future. If Christ has not been raised, you are wasting your time. Paul says, "If Christ has not been raised . . . then those also who have fallen asleep in Christ are lost" (1 Corinthians 15:17,18). There is no salvation, no hope for the future. Your death clock is ticking, and this broken world is all you get—along with bills, arthritis, watching your loved ones die, losing your hair (some of us quicker than others), standing in line at Walmart, sitting in traffic. If there is no resurrection, then life is just a cosmic joke. About 150,000 people die every day, and they are all just a bunch of nobodies along with you because there is nothing beyond the grave. You'd better have as much as you can because you will be worm food in a few years.

"Christ has indeed been raised from the dead, the firstfruits of those who have fallen asleep" (1 Corinthians 15:20). Christ was the first, and we will follow! His resurrection changes your eternal future. Jesus said, "I will not leave you as orphans; I will come to you. Before long, the world will not see me anymore, but you will see me. Because I live, you also will live" (John 14:18,19). Because of Jesus' resurrection, we will live new, eternal lives as God's somebodies forever with Jesus. We will talk about this a bit more at the end of the book.

What it means right now is that you have a brand-new life as God's somebody. You can start over completely. A few years ago, a 44-year-old man in Australia decided to auction off his life on eBay. His marriage had broken up, and he wanted to start over completely. He wrote, "Hi there, my name is Ian Usher, and I have had enough of my life! I don't want it anymore! You can have it if you like!" His life auction included not only his house, a car, a motorbike, a jet ski, and a spa but also an introduction to great friends and his job at a rug shop for a trial two-week period. "When it's over, I will just walk out the front door, take my wallet, my passport and start a new life," he said. Do you ever wish you could start over? To go from being a nobody with a lot of baggage to a fresh start, another chance to be somebody? That's the gift of Jesus' resurrection: a new life, now and forever. You are innocent before God and accepted as his precious child. You are not a victim of sin and Satan anymore. You have a blessed future on this earth, and even more in heaven.

The Resurrection Gets Personal

*Now, this is what the L*ORD *says—he who created you, Jacob, he who formed you, Israel: "Do not fear, for I have redeemed you; I have summoned you by name; you are mine."*

—Isaiah 43:1

I recently saw a cell phone case that looked like a bright yellow Pikachu, complete with a lightning tail and long, pointy ears that stuck one or two inches above the phone itself (incredibly cute, completely impractical). It's all about personalization—I want a cell phone case that fits me as much as the phone and makes a statement about my passions, my hobbies, or my worldviews. With the arrival of 3D printers and digitized everything, you can personalize almost anything you want nowadays—T-shirts with your family's coat of arms, keychains with a picture of your fuzzy teacup terrier, bobbleheads, socks, and jewelry. I was on a photo processing website the other day, and it offered to turn some of my personal photos into a throw blanket! But honestly, I don't know if I want to be sleeping under something that renders my grandkid's head the size of the Great Pumpkin.

Whether it's letter openers or coffee mugs, you can get it personalized. But what about your faith? What do I mean, you ask? Well, Jesus loves the world, but does he love me, personally? Jesus died for the world and rose from the grave for the eternal benefit of the world, but does he personally care about me? Or am I just lumped in with the crowd, like another can of beans in an aisle full of vegetables? It matters because I have real struggles and real feelings of shame and real moments of despair and frustration. I need to know if the God who died and rose and reigns forever on the throne of heaven really cares about nobodies like me, if the changes brought about by Jesus' resurrection apply specifically and personally to me.

The account of Mary Magdalene on the first Easter is a reminder that Jesus' resurrection gets personal. Before becoming one of Jesus' traveling companions who cared for him and his other disciples, Mary had been possessed by seven demons. In a culture where sickness and infirmity were assumed to be God's punishment for your disobedience, she was probably classified as a *sinner*, someone deservingly excluded from God's kingdom. Add to this the fact that she had been the habitation of seven maniacal monsters who likely drove her insane, and she was the kind of person that people went out of their way to avoid.

But Jesus not only had cleansed her body and soul, he also personally valued her and treasured her in a culture where women were second-class citizens. Who had ever heard of a rabbi accepting women into his entourage of disciples? Women were to be seen and not heard. Yet Jesus' followers included a whole group of females. Besides that, he was the first person to ever really give her hope: not just some temporary dream that she could be politically free or make a lot of money or look young for ten more years but eternal hope. It was the hope that someday helpless women wouldn't be plagued by demons or sidelined in society anymore, that God would wipe away her shame for good, and that she would be welcomed into his presence forever.

But when Jesus gasped for the last time on that rugged cross, Mary's hope faded like breath on a mirror, and she was back to being a nonentity—just another second-class citizen with no real future in ancient Palestine. Have you ever really gotten your hopes up about somebody only to have them dashed by reality? You were sure he was the one, but then he turned out to be a liar and a cheat. You seemed to be fitting in with the group, but then one of the other kids started making jokes at your expense, and you found yourself alone yet again.

You just knew that you and your new boss would get on famously, but he turned out to be an unbalanced slave driver. That's where Mary found herself. Jesus certainly had not been cruel or abusive, but that didn't change the fact that he was gone for good—a lot of too-big-to-be-true promises seemingly broken.

So on the third day after Jesus' death, Mary went to the tomb early in the morning because she still loved Jesus for all that he had done for her, but it was only to prepare his silent corpse for a better burial.

> Now Mary stood outside the tomb crying. As she wept, she bent over to look into the tomb and saw two angels in white, seated where Jesus' body had been, one at the head and the other at the foot.
> They asked her, "Woman, why are you crying?"
> "They have taken my Lord away," she said, "and I don't know where they have put him." At this, she turned around and saw Jesus standing there, but she did not realize that it was Jesus.
> He asked her, "Woman, why are you crying? Who is it you are looking for?"
> Thinking he was the gardener, she said, "Sir, if you have carried him away, tell me where you have put him, and I will get him."
> Jesus said to her, "Mary."
> She turned toward him and cried out in Aramaic, "Rabboni!" (which means "Teacher"). (John 20:11-16)

In nearly all other cases when angels appeared in the Bible, the people who saw them were terrified, but Mary was so blinded by her tears that she barely noticed these heavenly creatures. Come on! She didn't find it a little strange that two men dressed in dazzling white happened to be hanging out in an empty tomb? Not the normal place to play a round of cribbage and sip tea. That was the miserable intensity of her sorrow. In fact, Mary's heart was so dashed with disappointment that she couldn't even see her resurrected Savior when he was standing right in front of her. She was a hopeless mess.

Until that one simple word: "Mary." It's one thing to hear a tired voice call out your name at the DMV; it's quite another thing to have a loved one speak your name affectionately when your heart is suffocating on loneliness. Jesus didn't call her "woman" or "friend" or "disciple," but "Mary," by her own name, to remind her that he had personally come back from the dead for her.

Mark 16:9 tells us that Mary was the first person to witness the resurrected Jesus. There were a lot of people he could have appeared to first, a lot of people you would have expected him to appear to before Mary Magdalene—the 11 disciples, for example, the men he would soon send out to change the world. He could have appeared to the Jewish religious leaders who had scorned his message or the Roman governor who had condemned him to salvage a spiraling career. He could have appeared to his own mother to comfort her after she had seen her son unjustly torn to shreds. He could have appeared to hundreds of Jerusalem citizens from the top of the temple wall to make them think long and hard about demanding for his crucifixion. But instead, he chose to appear first to Mary Magdalene.

Do you remember when you would get these dubious offers in the mail: "You may have just won $1,000,000"? Every time I stood up on my tippy-toes and pulled one of those envelopes out of the mailbox, I must have handed it to my mother with dollar signs in my eyes like an old Bugs Bunny cartoon character. Just think of all the *Star Wars* action figures I could buy with a million dollars! Maybe I could finally get Kenner's Death Star Space Station (complete with foam-filled trash compactor)! I should have been a bit suspicious when I noticed that those letters were always addressed to my father or "Current Resident." And as a rule, our last name was misspelled, because there are only a handful of Doeblers in the entire world, and nobody knows how to spell German names correctly anyway. Why couldn't I have been a Smith?

Many of us think of Jesus' love in terms of "Mr. Smith, or Current Resident." We know that Jesus loves the world, and we are part of the world, of course. So Jesus must love us. Yet Jesus doesn't just love people in general like a politician claims to love the faceless masses of his constituency. He loves you specifically—by name, pimples, cowlicks, big toes, and all—just like he loved Mary. God so loved the world, but he also loves Mary and Matt and Christine and Madeline and Samuel and Caleb. As my sister-in-law likes to say, "I'm his favorite kid!"

That's what I love about Baptism and the Lord's Supper. When a pastor preaches from the pulpit, he tells the whole congregation, "Jesus loves you; Jesus died for you; Jesus rose for you." Yet the person who is pestered by a smothering sense of shame doesn't hear "you" as a *singular* pronoun. He hears it as a *plural* pronoun, and somehow, he figures that the pastor is speaking to everyone else but him. I don't know how it happens. It doesn't make any sense, but I'm telling you that's what happens. And if you have had this experience, then you know what I am talking about. The rest of you will just have to trust me.

However, in Baptism, God personalizes the glorious news of Jesus' resurrection for you: You yourself have been declared innocent before God; you yourself are empowered for a life of following Jesus; you yourself are guaranteed to rise again and live forever with him. The great missionary Paul put it this way, "We were therefore buried with him through baptism into death in order that, just as Christ was raised from the dead through the glory of the Father, we too may live a new life" (Romans 6:4). When Jesus died, it was as if you—singular—died to pay for your own sins. And when Jesus rose from the dead, he raised you—singular—up from the dead to give you a brand-new life of eternal hope and peace. Through Baptism, God personally carried you through that whole process; he personalized the glorious results of the resurrection for you. I love what Pastor Mark Jeske says about this: "The incredible events of Holy Week are not only a great drama for us to watch, passively admiring and worshiping Jesus Christ for what he pulled off. Your baptism actually connects you to Christ and puts you into the story."[29]

---

[29] Mark Jeske, *Restart: Promises new every morning to jump-start your day* (Milwaukee: Straight Talk Books, 2017), Kindle file, April 8.

When Jesus said that the Son of Man came "to give his life as a ransom for many" (Matthew 20:28), you were included in that "many." But in Communion, he says to you personally, "Take and eat; this is my body, given for you." You individually, you specifically, eat the bread and drink the wine. You personally taste and see that when Jesus died on the cross and rose from the grave, it wasn't just for the world; it was for you. You are forgiven and accepted. If you were the only sinful nobody in the universe, he still would have clambered up Calvary, carrying your cross. His Father is your Father. You are his somebody. "Sure, it's true for millions of other Christians out there. But right now, I want you to know that it's true for you, so take and eat; taste your forgiveness." The resurrected Savior is your personal Savior!

You can have your personalized keychain. I will take personalized water, bread, and wine—beautiful assurances that the resurrection of the Greatest Somebody who ever existed is, in fact, your resurrection. It doesn't get any more personal than that.

The Nobody Nobody Wanted

His love for you is never a result of your character; it is a clear demonstration of his.

—Paul David Tripp,
New Morning Mercies

We never know how good we can look, how delightful we can feel or how strong we can be until we hear ourselves addressed in love by God or by the one who represents God's love to us.

—Eugene H. Peterson,
Five Smooth Stones for Pastoral Ministry

Bam, bam, bam! We heard pounding on the front door at 1 A.M., early on a Sunday. I stumbled around in the dim light and answered it only to discover a very drunk man who wanted to talk. Since I was half-asleep and he was fully drunk, the conversation was almost comical, especially because it was in Chinese—one of us was slurring the language, the other was stumbling through—you figure out who was who. Finally, it became clear to me that he was asking if he could sit down. Given the circumstances, that was not a good idea, so I asked him if we could talk another time. He tried to show me where he lived but pointed in all four directions and mumbled something about Building 3. I asked him for his contact information, but he had lost his phone. As I escorted him out, I noticed that the floor of the entryway was covered in vomit. I watched him stumble to the elevator and get in. In the morning, I noticed that he must have come back out of the elevator, took off his jacket, thrown up some more, and then, apparently, urinated on the wall.

"That's disgusting," you say. "Do you really have to share this?" Yes, I do, because some great things happened through this rather unfortunate situation. First of all, I learned even more about the beautiful heart of my wife, Christine. Our entryway was public. People regularly walked through there. In fact, our landlord lived just across the hall from us at that time. Without a single complaint, my wife put on her rubber boots and dish gloves and cleaned up the whole mess on her hands and knees. She never said one negative thing about this bozo who scared us half to death and then made a disgusting mess all over our hallway. To me, it was a living picture of God's radical commitment to us.

Radical commitment

We learn more about the endless length of God's radical commitment to us through the little Bible book of Hosea. Around 760 b.c., Hosea was a prophet to God's people in Israel. Most pastors and prophets are supposed to use illustrations when they preach sermons; God decided to make this prophet into one:

> When the Lord began to speak through Hosea, the Lord said to him, "Go, marry a promiscuous woman and have children with her, for like an adulterous wife this land is guilty of unfaithfulness to the Lord." So he married Gomer daughter of Diblaim, and she conceived and bore him a son. (Hosea 1:2,3)

This is one of the most shocking commands God ever gave one of his prophets: marry a woman known around the town for promiscuity. She was the town floozy, maybe even a prostitute. People must have thought he was either nuts or a pervert. What kind of man of God does that?

God also said, "I want you to marry her knowing that she is going to cheat on you and cause you great pain." Hosea was a good prophet, so he did what God commanded, regardless of the cost. The intimations of her unfaithfulness started early. She bore three children. For the first one the Bible says she "bore him a son." But Hosea 1:6 says she "conceived again and gave birth to a daughter." And verse 8 says, "Gomer had another son." The second and third kids do not appear to be Hosea's, and it seems from the rest of the account that she repeatedly cheated on him.

God wanted Hosea to be an illustration of his radical commitment to the Israelite nation. God didn't choose his people because of their great potential; he chose them because of his grace, and he promised to love them forever like a faithful husband. In fact, he acted like the Israelites had been a beautiful treasure from the very beginning, even though the Bible reveals that they were a spiritual mess before, during, and after God declared them to be his "holy nation." Hosea 9:10 says, "When I found Israel, it was like finding grapes in the desert; when I saw your ancestors, it was like seeing the early fruit on the fig tree." Maybe you've heard the old saying: "He saw in her what no one else did." God flat-out saw something in the people that wasn't there. However, he didn't wait for them to become lovable before loving them; he loved them to make them lovable.

The same is true for us. God doesn't love you when you become lovable; he loves you long before that. People think they have to clean up before they come to God or go to church, but that's like a surgeon telling the patient in need of a triple bypass to run 30 miles before he will do the open-heart surgery. God says just the opposite. Come dirty, messy, hopeless—come, all you nobodies. God takes you as you are. In fact, no perfect people are allowed, that is, those pretending to have it all together. That's radical commitment.

God intended for there to be mutual commitment between himself and his people. However, in spite of his faithful love, the Israelites continually prowled about for other lovers. The nations around them worshiped fertility gods, a twisted form of religion that involved temple prostitution. Those nations weren't burdened with the boredom of holiness; it was anything goes, whatever works for them. So even though God's people were extremely prosperous under his boundless blessing, they left him for other lovers—the ancient Craigslist just offered too many opportunities for a "good time."

Gomer deserted Hosea repeatedly in her unfaithfulness, and when the consequences of her philandering were too costly and painful, she would drag herself back home because something was better than nothing (Hosea 2:7). Like Gomer, the Israelites occasionally would drag themselves to the Jerusalem temple to make offerings and say their prayers when life was less than ideal. God was the ace up their sleeves in case they needed a favor, the divine vending machine when they needed to snack on grace. They kept God's contact in their favorites for any real emergency. He knew the people were often using him, but like Hosea, he always took them back. That's radical commitment.

At the same time, God was not a fool. In love, he promised harsh discipline if they kept up this destructive cycle, because he knew their current path could only end in eternal sorrow. So he made Hosea name his children as warnings. The first child was named Jezreel after a city where there had been a horrible slaughter. It's like calling your son Dachau or Hiroshima. The warning? This is what will happen to you if you don't repent. The second child was named Lo-Ruhamah, which means "not loved." The warning? I will no longer show you love if you do not repent. The third child was named Lo-Ammi, which means "not my people." The warning? If you do not repent, I will divorce you. You will no longer be my people; you will no longer have my blessing and protection. Then see how far you get. Imagine what that was like for Hosea to call his children home in the evening: "Hey, Slaughter, Not-Loved, and Not-My-People, time for dinner!" Pretty weird. Yet their names were an illustration of what was waiting for God's people if they didn't repent.

Grace for Gomers

I'm a Gomer. We all are. We are nobodies by nature who have cheated repeatedly on God, especially we who follow him and—in one sense—know better. For example, we like to play at *church* so long as it's not too inconvenient. "Hey, God, let's hang out on Sunday—I dig the songs most of the time, except when they are played too slow, too fast, too loud, or too soft. I also really appreciate the sermon, especially if it's not too long or too short. I really enjoy this hour together; the rest of the week, I'll call you if I need anything. Oh, and can you make all the stoplights green while you're at it? After all, I'm running late for work. Please don't ask me to change too much, bring my junk into the light and deal with it, or sacrifice excessively for others. I'm busy, you know." I know this sounds crass, but things like this go through my mind in weaker moments.

That doesn't sound like much of a commitment on my part. And it's not what God is after either. Jesus says:

> Anyone who loves their father or mother more than me is not worthy of me; anyone who loves their son or daughter more than me is not worthy of me. Whoever does not take up their cross and follow me is not worthy of me. Whoever finds their life will lose it, and whoever loses their life for my sake will find it. (Matthew 10:37-39)

We might think, *Gee, that's awfully demanding,* but God expects this radical commitment because he created us and knows that our real, ultimate joy is found in him alone. If that sort of commitment seems ridiculous to you, think about marriage. Would you be happy if your spouse was only 25 percent faithful? What about 50 percent? Okay, what about 90 percent faithful—if he or she cheated on you only 10 percent of the time? Would that be acceptable? No. Because we instinctively know that the greatest joy and fulfillment in marriage only happens when spouses give themselves fully to each other, when there is a radical and exclusive commitment to each other. Unfaithfulness fractures the relationship; it gashes both parties.

So am I saying God wants us to go to church more, give more money, pray more, and do something nice for other people? No, he is saying that he wants all of you: 100 percent commitment. Your whole life: Monday through Sunday. As Jesus said, the greatest commandment is this: "Love the Lord your God with all your heart and with all your soul and with all your mind" (Matthew 22:37). Love him completely, radically.

Maybe that still sounds to some like a ploy for God to manipulate, control, and dominate us, but look again at the picture of God's radical commitment through Hosea.

> The LORD said to me, "Go, show your love to your wife again, though she is loved by another man and is an adulteress. Love her as the LORD loves the Israelites, though they turn to other gods and love the sacred raisin cakes." So I bought her for fifteen shekels of silver and about a homer and a lethek of barley. Then I told her, "You are to live with me many days; you must not be a prostitute or be intimate with any man, and I will behave the same way toward you." (Hosea 3:1-3)

Gomer cheats, then comes back; cheats, then comes back. Who knows how long this tragic cycle repeated itself. But one day she was gone for good. The closet was empty; two suitcases were missing; she had moved in with her lover. And apparently, she was working as a prostitute now because Hosea has to buy her back.

But this was more than the price of a good time with a woman; Hosea actually buys her back for good. Thirty shekels (silver pieces) was the price of a slave, the price to purchase a person. However, it appears that poor Hosea doesn't have 30 shekels, so he has to barter the rest of her cost with grain. This is mind-boggling! God doesn't send his heavenly Visa card or the magical money fairy to help Hosea pay that huge amount. He just tells Hosea to go get Gomer back and love her again. So Hosea is scraping up money on a prophet's salary—probably not $150 per hour plus a dental plan and four weeks of vacation—to buy back that whore of a wife who never really wanted to marry him in the first place. And I don't think it was all forced either. Notice in verse 1 that God says, "Go, show *your love* to your wife again" (emphasis mine). Apparently, Hosea had actually fallen in love with this wandering, unfaithful wife. That's radical commitment!

That's an illustration of God's commitment to you. Here's an interesting fact: The Jewish name Hosea, or Hoshea, is yet another rendering of the name Joshua, which is Jesus in Greek. So Hosea and

Jesus also have the same name. And Jesus would also pay an incredibly high price, infinitely more than 30 pieces of silver, to win us back from sin, death, and hell. That's the radical commitment of the cross. He was willing to pay whatever it took to get you back.

Pastor Matt Chandler tells about a time he went to a large concert for youth where another pastor spoke on the topic of sex. As a visual illustration, the speaker brought out a beautiful red rose. He smelled it, and then he threw it into the audience of a thousand high school and college kids. He told them to pass it around and smell it for themselves. While that was going on, he preached law and condemnation and what horrible diseases and consequences await those who are sexually promiscuous. At the end of his ranting, he asked, "Where's my rose?" Needless to say, when he received it back, it was all mangled: leaves broken, petals lost. Then he lifted it up, asking, "Now, who would want this rose?" implying that nobody would ever want to marry someone who had been sexually promiscuous. Matt says that, in frustration, he wanted to scream out, "Jesus wants the rose!" That is the point of the gospel, the good news of the Bible. Jesus wanted so badly to love all the mangled roses of the world that he paid the ultimate price. He let himself be trampled under our shame to the point that no one wanted him—not even his heavenly Father it seemed. "We thought his troubles were a punishment from God, a punishment for his own sins! But he was pierced for our rebellion, crushed for our sins. He was beaten so we could be whole. He was whipped so we could be healed. All of us, like sheep, have strayed away. We have left God's paths to follow our own. Yet the Lord laid on him the sins of us all" (Isaiah 53:4-6 New Living Translation).

It doesn't matter who you are or what a whore or worthless piece of trash you think you are. It doesn't matter how far you have run away from his goodness or how irresponsible, stupid, or wasteful you are—Jesus wants the rose. He wants you to know his grace, peace, and hope forever. Hosea lovingly said to Gomer, "I will live with you." Jesus has also said, "I will be with you always to the very end of the world." And beyond. That is radical commitment. And it's yours. He loves you not because you are somebody, but because he is. In fact, on the cross he became a nobody so it could honestly be said of you: You are the nobody that Nobody (Jesus) wants, just like Gomer.

No matter what

One more thing about this radical love. It must have been hard for Gomer to accept that she was really loved after all she had done and all that was done to her. She knew that she was a nobody better than anybody else, but Hosea did not see her that way. God does not see you that way either. You are not just an ugly, mangy puppy that God begrudgingly snatched off the street, at least not the way he sees you through Christ. Consider the words of Ephesians 5:25-27: "Husbands, love your wives, just as Christ loved the church and gave himself up for her to make her holy, cleansing her by the washing with water through the word, and to present her to himself as a radiant church, without stain or wrinkle or any other blemish, but holy and blameless." Those of you who have been sexually abused or sexually broken in some way probably need to hear that most of all: *completely cleansed.* You are not dirty or damaged goods to him. He transformed you into a *radiant* church—literally, "glorious, in great esteem, of high repute; illustrious, honorable, esteemed"—red carpet material. He transformed you into the model spouse without stain or wrinkle or any other blemish, but holy (he says it a second time), even blameless. In other words, Jesus' work on the cross is so complete that this is how God sees you now.

You might say, "But I don't see myself that way." It doesn't matter; how he sees you is what really matters. Notice in the previous reading: "to present her *to himself*" (emphasis mine). Think of all the time that most brides put into getting ready for their wedding day. They comb the city hunting for the perfect dress. They spend big money on professional nails, countless hours on the ideal hairstyle, sometimes using enough hairspray to create their own personal hole in the ozone, just to ensure that every strand is perfectly placed. Makeup, shoes—all of it down to the finest details. When we came to Jesus, we couldn't bring anything but dirty hands and unclean hearts. But through his death and resurrection, he presented us to himself in this way, even more perfect than the perfect bride. As one commentator put it, "Suffice it to say that as a result of what Christ did for his church, we are so completely holy that even the all-seeing eye of God can find nothing in us to hold against us."[30]

If you haven't noticed already, the Bible keeps repeating this good news relentlessly so that you will finally believe it. In the movie *Good Will Hunting,* Matt Damon plays Will, a genius who was severely abused as a child and has been in trouble with the law ever since. When Will finally agrees to get counseling to keep himself out of jail and able to stay with his girlfriend, he meets his counselor, Sean (Robin Williams). Sean tries to tell Will that the abuse he endured is not his fault, but there is still so much shame and anger that Will cannot accept this truth. The movie reaches its climax in an emotional exchange when Will stills seems stuck in a destructive cycle. Sean tells Will, "This is not your fault." Will nonchalantly responds, "Oh, I know." Again Sean says, "It's not your fault." Will smiles. "I know." "It's not your fault." "I know." "It's not your fault." Will, dead serious, replies, "I know." "It's not your fault." "Don't **** with me." Sean comes around the desk between them and sits in front of Will. "It's not your fault." The tears start. "I know." "It's not . . ." With tears flowing down his face, Will responds, "I know, I know."

All throughout Scripture, Jesus is telling you: "It's all forgiven . . ." "Oh, I know." "It's all forgiven." "I know." "It's all forgiven." "I know." "You can put down the fig leaf." "I know!" "You can stop restlessly laboring and rest in me." "I know!" "You can start a new day today." "I know!" "Nothing you do or don't do is going to change this." "I know!"

You just have to keep hearing it until you believe it. Because once you truly do believe it, it changes everything. If you are honored, cherished, loved, and forgiven like this, it transforms your whole perspective on life. It gives you a reason to live, to carry out God's purposes, to be who God made you to be.

---

[30] Irwin Habeck, *Ephesians* (Milwaukee: Northwestern Publishing House, 1985), p. 117.

Let me go back to the young man I mentioned at the beginning of this chapter. He showed up at my home later that day (after throwing up in our hallway twice) to apologize. I told him that we are Christians and that we forgive people. We gave him a Bible. We told him to read the gospel of Mark and send us any questions he had. He was shocked. We exchanged contact information, and I have had further opportunities to shower him with grace.

In the local language, his name could be translated as "bright promise." The night he banged on our door, there wasn't much bright promise to be seen—just a young man making a fool of himself, possibly in the midst of throwing his life away, but God used it to introduce him to the life-changing gospel. It turns out that the young man actually lives three floors above us, and his apartment door would be in the exact same spot and position as our door. For some reason, the elevator doors opened on our floor and brought us together as he stumbled to what he thought was his door. I like to think it is for his eternal good, the bright promise of heaven.

Part 4

Nobody's Business

When I think upon my God, my heart is so full that the notes dance and leap from my pen and since God has given me a cheerful heart, it will be pardoned me that I serve Him with a cheerful spirit.

—Franz Josef Haydn

People often say, "It's nobody's business what I do with my life." Actually, it is. It's God's business. First of all, he created you. Psalm 139 says, "You created my inmost being; you knit me together in my mother's womb. I praise you because I am fearfully and wonderfully made; your works are wonderful, I know that full well" (verses 13,14). Second, he redeemed you at the cost of his precious Son's blood. Missionary Paul writes, "You were bought at a price. Therefore honor God with your bodies" (1 Corinthians 6:20), and, "I urge you, brothers and sisters, in view of God's mercy, to offer your bodies as a living sacrifice, holy and pleasing to God—this is your true and proper worship" (Romans 12:1). You are twice God's: once because he made you, twice because he bought you.

And this God commands us to love others sacrificially in quiet service, especially the overlooked and overburdened of this world. This is our nobody business, a reflection of his priceless love for us. But what does that look like in our hectic lives today—right now?

Nobodies Are the Norm

It doesn't matter if the world knows, or sees or under-stands, the only applause we are meant to seek is that of nail-scarred hands.

> —Unknown author in R. Scott Rodin,
> *The Steward Leader: Transforming People, Organizations and Communities*

Such is oft the course of deeds that move the wheels of the world: small hands do them because they must, while the eyes of the great are elsewhere.

> —Elrond,
> *The Fellowship of the Ring*

I loved *The Lord of the Rings* trilogy when it wasn't cool in the 1980s, after the hippies moved on from it ("Frodo Lives!") and before Peter Jackson's movies came out—that in-between time when nerds who liked that stuff sometimes had their underwear pulled up over their heads (not that it ever happened to me; I'm just saying in theory). There weren't any cool *Lord of the Rings* video games. There was one game for kids based on *The Hobbit* where you rolled dice and moved around a board based on the number of pips you got; it made *Chutes and Ladders* look fun by comparison. There was one painful cartoon version of the book that featured the classic ditty "Where there's a whip, there's a way." There was a weird song by Rush about Rivendell, the hidden enclave of the elves. Leonard Nimoy crooned out a song about Bilbo Baggins, complete with a music video that makes you wonder if someone squirted hallucinogenic syrup in your Wheaties.

Thus, it might surprise you to find out that *The Lord of the Rings* (LotR) was voted the book of the century at the end of the 20th century, and it shows no signs of "sailing into the West" (that's nerd humor right there). It's been translated into 38 languages; over 150 million copies of it have been sold; new printings come out every few years. Why? LotR hits us right at home because it is about (you guessed it) nobodies. In fact, that is one of the major themes of the book—that great things are accomplished by the unlikeliest of heroes, ordinary folk that most of us can identify with.

The real heroes of LotR are not Gandalf, as cool as he is; or Galadriel, as majestic as she is; or Boromir, as noble as he is. The real heroes are Frodo and his companion, Sam. Sam is a peculiar hero—a short, chubby, minimally educated gardener who speaks with a Cockney accent. As he and Frodo make the dark trek to Mordor, he seems to spend most of his time huffin' and puffin', asking dumb questions, and dreaming about food. But in the end, he is the one who refuses to give up against insurmountable odds, who continues to see good in the darkest places, who carries Frodo up the side of a mountain to finish their quest. He's a nobody, but he accomplishes great things in quiet ways. There's a reason why one of my children is named Sam.

Our gracious God also has a propensity to accomplish great things through nobodies, often in quiet ways. In this chapter, I will take you on a brief tour of some Bible nobodies. They may be nameless, faceless people to the world, but God has written their names in the book of life and used them in powerful ways to advance his kingdom.

The nobody lists

If you need help falling asleep, some people might suggest you read the biblical genealogies. Be honest—when you see all those impossible-to-pronounce names in your Bible, you're tempted to scan them quicker than the entries in the Oxford English Dictionary.

What's the point of having them in the Bible? It's not like Moses or Matthew had to meet a required number of words for their Scripture-writing class in high school.[31] These nobodies may mean little to us today, but they mean something to God. Nobody would remember these nonentities otherwise, but God chose to ink them forever in his Holy Word. In some lists, he wants to show how they fit into the family tree of Jesus, known as the red line of the Savior. We will see an example of that in Rahab's life in the next chapter. God wants us to see that he was keeping his promise made to Adam and Eve that one of their descendants would crush the head of Satan. In other lists, he wants us to see how he used ordinary people to keep his kingdom work marching forward, like rebuilding the temple and the wall of Jerusalem.

Eugene Peterson says it beautifully:

> The genealogical lists in the Bible, synonymous in so many minds with tedium, are, in fact, documentation for the most exciting parts of the story. For the gospel does not address a faceless, nameless mob, but persons. The history of salvation is thick with names. The name is the form of speech by which a person is singled out for personal love, particular intimacy, and exact responsibilities. The biblical fondness for genealogical lists is not pedantic antiquarianism, it is a search for personal involvement, a quest for a sense of personal place in the web of relationships in which God fashions salvation.[32]

You may feel like a nobody in your family. Maybe your brother was the big sports star, and your sister was the popular one, and your dad

---

[31] Remember how we used to stop at 501 words when 500 words were required in an essay? It didn't matter if it was the middle of a sentence. We were done; requirement met.

[32] Eugene H. Peterson, *Five Smooth Stones for Pastoral Work* (Grand Rapids: Wm. B. Eerdmans Publishing Co., 1980), Kindle file, Chapter 2.

got a full ride to university. But you are also in the family line of Jesus through faith in him, and he has a place for you.

Read more: Genesis 5 and 10:21-32 and 11:10-26; Ezra 2; Nehemiah 3; Matthew 1:1-17; Luke 3:23-38.

Jonathan's armor-bearer

In *Star Wars: A New Hope*, Obi-Wan Kenobi says, "Who's the more foolish? The fool or the fool who follows him?" In the book of 1 Samuel, God's people are on the brink of bitter enslavement as the Philistine armies move to attack them. The situation is so critical that only Jonathan and his father, the king, have weapons in the entire Israelite army. Jonathan trusts God. So he says to his armor-bearer, "Let's you and I go attack that Philistine outpost. God will help us." The armor-bearer, who has no weapon, says, "I am with you heart and soul" (1 Samuel 14:7). At a time when many of the other soldiers had defected or were hiding in caves, the armor-bearer attacks. "Jonathan climbed up, using his hands and feet, with his armor-bearer right behind him. The Philistines fell before Jonathan, and his armor-bearer followed and killed behind him. In that first attack Jonathan and his armor-bearer killed some twenty men in an area of about half an acre" (1 Samuel 14:13,14). It's their attack that God uses to trigger panic in the Philistine army. The other Israelite soldiers are emboldened and rout the army of their enemies.

Sometimes, God calls us, seeming nobodies, to follow him into dangerous places, without any apparent weapon to defend ourselves or tools to accomplish what he is calling us to. But he goes before us like Jonathan; he defends us. He will bless us as we step out in faith.

Read more: 1 Samuel 14:1-23.

The Samaritan woman

She had been married five times, and the guy she was now with was not her husband. She lived in a small town. People talked. They all knew she was a floozy, someone to be avoided. But when Jesus changed her life with his gospel promises, she used her sinful past as a way to attract their attention: "Come, see a man who told me everything I ever did. Could this be the Messiah?" (John 4:29).

Jesus can use your brokenness to make a difference in the lives of others. Your failures and your wounds are just opportunities to point people to the One who knows everything you ever did but still loves you with an everlasting love.

Read more: John 4:4-42.

Cleopas

Who in the world is Cleopas? Not even many Christians know him. He's like Emmet in *The Lego Movie*—just another yellow plastic smiley face in a world of smiley faces. And Cleopas' companion doesn't even get a name. Yet Jesus appeared to these two guys on the evening of the first Easter. He walked for miles with them while patiently explaining to their stubborn hearts how he was the fulfillment of the Scriptures—how he needed to suffer, die, and rise from the dead. Didn't Jesus have more important things to do and more important people to talk to? Nope. These two nobodies had his full attention.

Sometimes, especially when we feel like nobodies, we are afraid to trouble Jesus in prayer. "He has enough going on without me pestering him. Besides, why would he listen to me?" Jesus loves to spend time with people whom some would consider nothing. Talk with him; he's listening.

Read more: Luke 24:13-35.

Shiphrah and Puah

I bet you haven't heard of these ladies either. Just a couple of nobody midwives. The king of Egypt (who is never named, much to the chagrin of archaeologists and historians) demanded that they kill any baby boy they helped birth as a way to control the Israelite population. But they trusted God and disobeyed the king even though it probably meant a death sentence for them. God blessed them for it and gave them families of their own. The population of Israel continued to thrive because of their efforts.

We are often afraid to do the right thing, to defend those who cannot defend themselves or stand up for the truth. After all, it may just bring a lot of trouble on us. We may lose our reputation; we may lose our jobs; we may lose our friends or even our family. But God promises to bless us with eternal rewards, as Paul says, "Our light and momentary troubles are achieving for us an eternal glory that far outweighs them all. So we fix our eyes not on what is seen, but on what is unseen, since what is seen is temporary, but what is unseen is eternal" (2 Corinthians 4:17,18).

Read more: Exodus 1:15-21.

The Colossian church

I went to see the ruins of Colossae in Turkey. It's just a big hill covered in grass and rocks. If you use your imagination, you can kind of see where the theater used to be. No archaeologists have bothered to excavate the city because it's just not that important, especially when compared to the other two famous ancient cities in the area, Hierapolis and Laodicea.

And yet the great missionary Paul wrote the Colossian Christians a letter, even though he never met them personally as far as we know. His letter to the Laodicean Christians didn't make it into the Bible, but the letter to the Colossian Christians did. A letter to a tiny church in a tiny city. Paul told them, "We always thank God, the Father of our Lord Jesus Christ, when we pray for you, because we have heard of your faith in Christ Jesus and of the love you have for all God's people" (Colossians 1:3,4).

Over the years, I have heard many Christians complain about their small church, as if they are embarrassed by it. There is nothing wrong with small churches. God is with them, and God works through them to make a big difference in the lives of the people around them. Don't make excuses for your tiny church. Don't look down on the others there—look for a way that you can serve to bless the brothers and sisters God has given you.

Read more: Colossians 1.

Hannah

Her husband was pretty insensitive; her husband's other wife scorned her; the priest accused her of being a drunk just because she was praying so earnestly that she was mumbling out loud. She was barren in a culture where the inability to have children was one of the worst curses a woman could experience, but it didn't stop her from trusting God. She prayed, put the results in God's hands, and moved on. God heard her prayer and granted her a son. In return, she offered that son, Samuel, as a servant of God for his entire life—she didn't feel the need to hang greedily on to a blessing that was never hers in the first place.

It's hard to keep trusting God when he doesn't seem to be answering our prayers. We start to doubt if we really are his. And when he does answer, we're tempted to hoard what we receive for ourselves, as if we had worked so hard for it. Hannah reminds us that God is always faithful, in plenty or in want. We can put the prayers, the answers, and our entire lives in his capable and loving hands.

Read more: 1 Samuel 1 and 2:1-10.

The sinful woman

The sinful woman doesn't even get a name in the Bible story about her. She is just "a sinful woman." Besides that, our lesson tells us that she was a sinner "in that town." Think small-town America where everyone knows what everyone had for breakfast. Everyone would have known her sordid history. She probably endured scornful looks from people every day.

She knew she was a nobody, but she also knew Jesus—and that's what gave her the courage to crash the party of an upstanding citizen and endure all those judgmental stares from the guests. That's what gave her the guts to cry on the feet of this famous rabbi and wipe his feet with her hair. She knew that, if anyone would accept her, it would be Jesus. She didn't care what other people thought about her or what they did to her. If Jesus was willing to accept her, what they said didn't matter.

If you are not worried about what others think or are not obsessed with impressing others because you know that Christ accepts you, you are truly free. You are free to do what is right because, if someone doesn't like it—well, who cares? You have Jesus. You are free to attempt great things because what's the worst that could happen to you? You could die, and then you would be ushered into the presence of your Savior, which is better by far.

Read more: Luke 7:36-50.

Ehud

Ehud was one of the judges who helped to deliver God's people in one of the darkest periods of their history. The Bible says that Ehud was left-handed and that, somehow, he snuck an 18-inch double-edged sword past the royal guards and into the throne room of Eglon, the monarch who was violently oppressing God's people. The Bible says the sword was strapped to his right thigh under his clothing. I don't know about you, but I would have some serious trouble walking normally if I had an 18-inch sword strapped to my leg. One theory is that Ehud was physically challenged and walked with a limp anyway. That would explain why no one was afraid to let the foreign emissary of an oppressed people meet alone with the king. No matter what, he wasn't seen as much of a threat, but Ehud plunged his sword into fat Eglon's belly, rallied his people, and delivered them from oppression.

Maybe you're disabled in some way, physically or emotionally. Maybe you struggle with depression or anxiety. Maybe you stutter. Maybe arthritis wracks your body so badly that some days you can barely get out of bed. God still has plans to work through you for his good purposes.

Read more: Judges 3:12-30.

Nobody heroes

Hebrews 11 is commonly referred to as the heroes of faith chapter. It starts out with people you would expect to see in a list of Bible heroes: Noah, Abraham, Joseph, and Moses. But then, there is this little list of nameless ones at the end:

> There were others who were tortured, refusing to be released so that they might gain an even better resurrection. Some faced jeers and flogging, and even chains and imprisonment. They were put to death by stoning; they were sawed in two; they were killed by the sword. They went about in sheepskins and goatskins, destitute, persecuted and mistreated—the world was not worthy of them. They wandered in deserts and mountains, living in caves and in holes in the ground. (Hebrews 11:35-38)

They have no names. They died in ignominy. No one remembers what they did. And God says, "The world was not worthy of them."

Some of the greatest people you will ever meet in your life will be people whose names nobody really knows, men and women who quietly and faithfully carry out the vocations they have been assigned. Listen to them and learn from them. Follow their godly example. Theirs is the real life.

Read more: Hebrews 11 and 12:1-3.

Naaman's slave girl

Bands of raiders from the godless country of Aram had stripped this girl of her freedom. It's possible she had been raped by her captors and humiliated in other ways after seeing her town pillaged and her loved ones murdered. She was a hopeless slave in a foreign country. Like many immigrant workers today, there was little chance of ever returning home to see her family and friends. She had every reason to hate her master, Naaman. After all, he was not only her foreign master, but he was also the commander-in-chief of the army who had raided her country. But when Naaman contracted leprosy, she was quick to offer help. She informed her owners that there was a prophet in Israel who could cure him. As a result of her astonishing act of mercy, Naaman was not only cured—he became a follower of the true God.

It's so difficult to forgive those who have made you feel like a nobody—that mother with her impossible demands, that brother who relentlessly teased you to make himself feel better, that Christian sister who ruined your reputation. And how could we ever dream of blessing or praying for people like that? Only through the God who continued to watch over his daughter in her slavery far from home. He who made you somebody special through Christ will help you through this too.

Read more: 2 Kings 5.

John Mark

John Mark is one of my favorite nobodies and a personal hero. He didn't get off to a great start. When Jesus was arrested, he appears to be the young man who wiggled out of his garment and fled naked (Mark 14:52). Later he went on a missionary journey with Paul and Barnabas but abandoned them at the first sign of hardship. Paul adamantly refused to take him on the next trip. And yet, many years later, Paul would write to his assistant Timothy, "Get Mark and bring him with you, because he is helpful to me in my ministry" (2 Timothy 4:11). And Mark would go on to write the gospel of Mark, a simple and straightforward account of the life of Jesus that has been instrumental in converting and strengthening hundreds of millions of Christians.

Maybe you made a fool of yourself. Maybe you failed multiple times in the past. It's okay. God uses nobodies like that to reach other struggling people. Your failures don't need to define you, but you can use them to prepare you for God's future work in your life.

Read more: the gospel of Mark.

Thinking smaller

Why does God use nobodies? Because when ordinary people are empowered by him to do extraordinary things, we are inspired to do the same with God's promises behind us. And then, when all is done well, our worthy God gets the glory. We don't get caught up in the cult of personality that surrounds great people. Instead, we look beyond the person to the God who is working through them, and we say, "What an awesome God we have!"

So get busy being an ordinary servant of the Lord. For years, especially in the church, we have talked about making a big difference. It's a good thing to think about changing the world, but sometimes, we set people up for failure if they can't do some great thing for God—at least what seems to be some great thing in the eyes of the world. Sometimes our big ideas are not so much about making a difference for Jesus as making a difference for us. It's not bad to dream big, but godly dreams start with being faithful with what's right in front of you.

As I mentioned before, maybe we have put too much pressure on our children by telling them, "You can do anything you want to." How much healthier would it be to tell them, "You can do what God calls you to do in your different vocations, because God strengthens those he calls. And if God gives you opportunities to do even more than that, seize the day! You may not become super famous or successful by the world's standards, but you will live a good life, one that gives glory to him and blesses the people he puts in your path."

Remember the story of Vinko Bogataj? Don't tell me you've forgotten him already? The skier who pinwheeled down the slope while everyone watched weekly for years on ABC's *Wide World of Sports*? As people rushed to help Vinko after his infamous spill, he told reporters that he immediately wanted to go back up and try again—which would have been his third attempt after two horrible falls (you don't get to see the first spill in the introduction). He was, understandably, rushed to the hospital instead. Later, he called from the hospital to tell everyone that he was fine and would be back again.

Many years later, at the 20th anniversary celebration of the *Wide World of Sports,* Vinko received a standing ovation. He had a huge grin on his face as he stood in the company of famous athletes like Peggy Fleming and Muhammad Ali, who was the first to get Vinko's autograph. Imagine that: a total nobody inspiring people and changing their lives. That's the way God works. He accomplishes big things through nobodies in quite ordinary ways.

Loving Nobodies

Make friends with nobodies; don't be the great somebody.

—Romans 12:16, *The Message*

I am pained by my graceless heart, my prayerless days, my poverty of love, my sloth in the heavenly race, my sullied conscience, my wasted hours, my unspent opportunities.

—A Puritan Prayer

In the early 1960s during the Vietnam War, the CIA recruited and trained Hmong hill tribesmen living in Laos to fight against the North Vietnamese Army. Apparently, the majority of the Hmong men joined this "secret army," and many made great sacrifices to assist the US armed forces.

But when American forces pulled out of Laos in 1973, the Laotian Hmong were in a dangerous position, facing reprisals and even possible extermination for their support of the United States. Tens of thousands of Hmong people fled to Thailand, trekking through the mountains or swimming across the Mekong River.

"Ying" was one of those refugees, an astonishingly courageous woman. She spent a whole night crossing the river from Laos to a refugee camp, pulling her family along by a rope as they clung to anything that would float because she was the only one who knew how to swim. She told how wicked opportunists would prowl about in boats, bashing helpless, floating refugees on the head with oars and stealing what meager possessions they still had.

She and her husband eventually immigrated to the United States and settled in the state of Wisconsin, where she bore seven children. Then her husband died suddenly while she was pregnant with her eighth.

Thankfully, God worked through a local Christian couple to minister to her and her precious children. They not only cared for the physical needs of this family, but they also shared the message of Jesus—the Savior who immigrated to our planet and spent most of his early years as a refugee in Egypt, hiding from a maniacal king. The Holy Spirit moved Ying to accept the good news about our humble Lord. And one Sunday, she and all eight of her children were baptized together, one right after the other. Nine castaway Hmong refugees were welcomed into God's family and that local congregation.

However, her new brothers and sisters in faith weren't always quite sure how best to serve her. She was a foreigner and a single mom with eight children; it was difficult to find common ground for building a relationship with her. Conversation with her was also difficult because her English level was basic and her accent was heavy at the time. Inviting her family over for dinner seemed like a huge investment. Even though her kids were always well behaved, there were eight of them! Would they like the traditional Midwestern dishes like tater tot casserole and burgers on the grill? Don't they eat rice noodles and egg rolls? What would you talk about? Would you say something wrong and offend her?

The first Hmong refugees began arriving in the United States in 1975 and settled primarily in the Midwest. By 2006, there were nearly 40,000 Hmong living in Wisconsin. In 2014, Hmong Americans made up the largest Asian ethnic group in the state. And yet, for many Midwestern Christians, the whole people group remained an enigma, even when they had lived among us for decades and were members of our own churches!

God has a special place in his heart for those who are sometimes overlooked or avoided, people like Ying and her precious children.

> "The Lord watches over the foreigner and sustains the fatherless and the widow." (Psalm 146:9)

> "But you, God, see the trouble of the afflicted; you consider their grief and take it in hand. . . . You are the helper of the fatherless." (Psalm 10:14)
>
> "He defends the cause of the fatherless and the widow, and loves the foreigner residing among you, giving them food and clothing." (Deuteronomy 10:18)

In the Bible, God repeatedly commands his people to imitate his love for these kinds of people.

> "Religion that God our Father accepts as pure and faultless is this: to look after orphans and widows in their distress." (James 1:27)
>
> "Do not deprive the foreigner or the fatherless of justice, or take the cloak of the widow as a pledge." (Deuteronomy 24:17)
>
> "At the end of every three years, bring all the tithes of that year's produce and store it in your towns, so that . . . the foreigners, the fatherless and the widows who live in your towns may come and eat and be satisfied, and so that the LORD your God may bless you in all the work of your hands." (Deuteronomy 14:28,29)

In this and many other passages, God calls his people to be the masks he wears to care for the overlooked and avoided. We are the hands and voice of God for those he wants to bless.

He sternly warns those who oppress these people he cherishes. "[The wicked] slay the widow and the foreigner; they murder the fatherless. They say, 'The LORD does not see; the God of Jacob takes no notice.' . . . Does he who fashioned the ear not hear? Does he who formed the eye not see? Does he who disciplines nations not punish?" (Psalm 94:6,7,9,10).

But he also sternly warns those who *ignore* these people he cherishes. "[The wicked among God's people] have grown fat and sleek. Their evil deeds have no limit; they do not seek justice. They do not promote the case of the fatherless; they do not defend the just cause of the poor" (Jeremiah 5:28). Notice that these folks were not actively oppressing the fatherless and the poor. They were not actively pulling the pigtails of dirty-faced orphans like Miss Hannigan did, but they weren't doing anything to help them either. Don't be deceived; God takes ignoring the underprivileged as seriously as actively oppressing them.

Loving like nobody else

The Bible tells us about one particular foreigner who had an extra-special place in God's heart (though it might shock you to know it): the prostitute Rahab. Rahab was a Canaanite, a despicable people group who desecrated their land (modern-day Israel) through an aberrant and disgusting religion built around fertility. Their places of worship often featured the Asherah pole, a giant phallus set on top of a hill in full view of every man, woman, and child living within a few miles. Male and female prostitutes served as the priests and priestesses of these torrid temples. It's quite possible Rahab herself participated in their demonic liturgies and regularly offered her body and soul as a living sacrifice to the vile pagan gods of her country.

As God's people entered this bleak land, they knew they would have to conquer its pagan inhabitants, people like Rahab. And one of the centers of their power was located in Jericho.

> Then Joshua son of Nun secretly sent two spies from Shittim. "Go, look over the land," he said, "especially Jericho." So they went and entered the house of a prostitute named Rahab and stayed there.
> The king of Jericho was told, "Look, some of the Israelites have come here tonight to spy out the land." So the king of Jericho sent this message to Rahab: "Bring out the men who came to you and entered your house, because they have come to spy out the whole land."
> But the woman had taken the two men and hidden them. She said, "Yes, the men came to me, but I did not know where they had come from. At dusk, when it was time to close the city gate, they left. I don't know which way

they went. Go after them quickly. You may catch up with them." (But she had taken them up to the roof and hidden them under the stalks of flax she had laid out on the roof.) So the men set out in pursuit of the spies on the road that leads to the fords of the Jordan, and as soon as the pursuers had gone out, the gate was shut.

Before the spies lay down for the night, she went up on the roof and said to them, "I know that the LORD has given you this land and that a great fear of you has fallen on us, so that all who live in this country are melting in fear because of you. We have heard how the LORD dried up the water of the Red Sea for you when you came out of Egypt, and what you did to Sihon and Og, the two kings of the Amorites east of the Jordan, whom you completely destroyed. When we heard of it, our hearts melted in fear and everyone's courage failed because of you, for the LORD your God is God in heaven above and on the earth below. "Now then, please swear to me by the LORD that you will show kindness to my family, because I have shown kindness to you. Give me a sure sign that you will spare the lives of my father and mother, my brothers and sisters, and all who belong to them—and that you will save us from death."

"Our lives for your lives!" the men assured her. "If you don't tell what we are doing, we will treat you kindly and faithfully when the LORD gives us the land."

So she let them down by a rope through the window, for the house she lived in was part of the city wall. (Joshua 2:1-15)

Important question: Did God spare Rahab because he owed her a favor? She had undoubtedly ruined marriages and contributed to the breakdown of society through her ungodly occupation. She had almost certainly been a willing participant in her vile religion. One simple act of kindness does not level a mountain of rebellious rubble. Yet this going-nowhere nobody gets written into the story of God's people.

That was only the beginning of his gracious work to exalt this foreigner. She is the only woman besides Abraham's wife Sarah to make the heroes of faith list in Hebrews 11 where it says, "By faith the prostitute Rahab, because she welcomed the spies, was not killed with those who were disobedient" (verse 31). Notice how she is contrasted with those who were disobedient, as if she were a model citizen. The book of James even puts her in the same category as Abraham, that of a righteous person, something that must have shocked his Jewish readers. A gentile prostitute presented as an equal with the father of the Jews?

God's love for this foreign woman was so intense that it even rubbed off on his people. The spies' treatment of Rahab is remarkable. These men had been raised on stories of just how wicked the Canaanites were. And yet, without any permission from their superiors or thought for what others might think, these soldiers put their reputations and necks on the line to spare a disreputable woman and her family. They treated her as a soul, not as a nuisance, a problem, a statistic, or a drain on their time. The result was that she was welcomed into the family on their recommendation.

And Rahab was not tucked away in some corner like an eccentric auntie whom no one knows what to do with. The author of Joshua wrote that she "lives among the Israelites to this day" (6:25). In fact, Matthew 1:5 tells us that a righteous man named Salmon married her. It didn't matter to him what she had been before. She was one of them now. She was not an outsider or a lesser citizen, but a true member of the family—just as much as the godly woman who could trace her bloodlines all the way back to the great patriarch Judah.

God's people in the Old Testament didn't always do so great when it came to their interactions with outsiders. They had a difficult time maintaining the godly middle path of acceptance without approval, the path of kindness and compassion toward those who had lost their way, regardless of their backstory. But in the case of Rahab, they really shined.

Then God crowned this whole redemptive story by honoring Rahab even further. Rahab and Salmon had a son named Boaz, another righteous man who married another outsider—Ruth. That means that Rahab was the great-great-grandmother of King David, and in his gospel, Matthew proudly informs us that she was an ancestor of Jesus. God didn't just tolerate Rahab—he wove her into his salvation story by blood. Your Jewish Savior has a little bit of Canaanite blood in him because of Rahab. There is a place of honor for Rahab in the family of God next to the greats like Boaz, Ruth, David, and Jesus.

Today, God calls us to love those who are overlooked and avoided in the same way. But it is super difficult! My biggest challenge is that I myself often overlook them because of busy-ness or thoughtless distraction. I remember one time my family and I were leaving a concert in the city late at night. The traffic was bumper to bumper; we were waiting at a stoplight for what seemed like an eternity. The kids were cranky. I was stressed. Suddenly from the backseat Maddie asked me timidly, "Dad, do we have any food?" I yelled at her, "I don't have any food! It's late at night! You don't need to eat now!" With a trembling voice she responded, "I was just wondering if we had something to give that homeless man there." She was referring to the shabby beggar whom I had been ignoring as he went from idling car to idling car, holding out his chapped and filthy hands in a plea. Once again, Maddie noticed someone I had overlooked. Whom do you overlook? We often love those who are easier to love and dismiss the others as someone else's responsibility.

To be honest, in many similar situations, I haven't overlooked the person so much as avoided them, because I am afraid of awkward moments. You might know the drill: Look straight ahead and avoid eye contact. Pretend you don't see them. Take the long way around to avoid getting too close. Ignore that text or that friend invite because you don't need the extra hassle. Make up vague commitments and calendar events to excuse yourself from uncomfortable situations with certain people.

Because of my dear wife's compassion, we have had many interesting interactions with people who are regularly overlooked and avoided. A homeless family of 11 stayed with us for a few days when they had nowhere to go. I still remember Christine making about 20 grilled-cheese sandwiches and stewing up a giant pot of tomato soup for them. As she handed the mother a sandwich and a bowl of soup, this homeless woman replied, "Oh, I'm not really a soup and sandwich kind of girl." Here my wife was slaving over a feast for this homeless family and the mom had the gall to turn her nose up at the food. That was awkward.

A recovering heroin addict who had been a prostitute lived with us for a bit. There were some awkward moments.

We invited a Hindu couple to our house because they were fairly new to the United States and feeling a bit overwhelmed. We weren't quite sure what they could eat according to their beliefs, so Christine settled on veggie lasagna. We weren't sure how we should handle the dinner prayer or how exactly to respond when the wife finished singing a song of praise to Vishnu. There were some awkward moments.

I remember Christine inviting the friend of a friend to come over to our house to play board games. That friend brought her boyfriend, who was sporting a T-shirt praising the devil for something or other. It was not a New Jersey Devils jersey; it was not a Tasmanian Devil from Bugs Bunny kind of T-shirt; it was not a polo for a Dirt Devil vacuum cleaner salesperson. It was an actual "U-ra-ra, Devil" kind of shirt. That was a bit awkward.

I know it's uncomfortable sometimes, but God wants us to push through the awkwardness to love these people he deeply cherishes.

Learning from nobody

Of course, when we read Rahab's story, we probably think of the kindness it must have taken for Joshua, the spies, and the Israelites to take this foreigner in, especially given her background. But they were God's people; we might expect this sort of behavior from them.

Rahab, on the other hand, exhibits astonishing faith and grace, even though she had only been a God-follower for a few days. To this point in her life, she had been a pagan. She slept with men for money, probably participating regularly in the ritual sex of the vile

Canaanite religion. And yet, she now confessed, "The LORD your God is God in heaven above and on the earth below"—not just another local deity but the only true God over all creation. She also said, "I *know* that the LORD has given you this land." This spiritual infant had more faith than the ten Israelite spies who had been sent into the land 40 years earlier and convinced God's people that conquering it was too difficult. Still more, she risked her life for a couple of foreigners she didn't know. When she shared the news about the spies with her family members, they could have turned her in for collusion with the enemy. She even encouraged Joshua and the spies with her words. A prostitute! A new believer, filled with faith and courage! First Corinthians 1:26-29 says:

> Brothers and sisters, think of what you were when you were called. Not many of you were wise by human standards; not many were influential; not many were of noble birth. But God chose the foolish things of the world to shame the wise; God chose the weak things of the world to shame the strong. God chose the lowly things of this world and the despised things—and the things that are not—to nullify the things that are, so that no one may boast before him.

Rahab was less than a nobody among the people of faith, and yet she was a great example to them.

When we work up the courage to reach out to those who are generally overlooked and avoided, it is easy to do so from a position of superiority. Perhaps we feel required to help them because they can't get their stuff together like normal people. Perhaps we secretly thank God that we would never have allowed ourselves to stoop so low. We probably don't deliberately set out to feel superior to them, but it happens. When we think of certain people only as nobodies who need our help, we tend to view ourselves as reaching down to lift them up. And we have difficulty imagining ourselves being lifted up by them.

We must remind ourselves that there really are no nobodies from God's point of view. I love the way C. S. Lewis put it in his sermon

"The Weight of Glory": "There are no *ordinary* people. You have never talked to a mere mortal. Nations, cultures, arts, civilizations—these are mortal, and their life is to ours as the life of a gnat. But it is immortals whom we joke with, work with, marry, snub and exploit." Every person you see—whether wealthy or destitute, stunningly beautiful or cringingly ugly, wildly successful or a hopeless flop—is a soul whom Jesus knit together in the womb and for whom he sacrificed his life.

And through the Holy Spirit, God is weaving within this person a unique perspective and blessing to offer the church. Andrew Peterson writes, "Your story, then, is yours and no one else's. Each sunset is different, depending on where you stand. . . . This is part of my calling—to make known the heart of God. And because he holds a special place in his heart for me and me alone (just as he holds a special place for you), my story stands a chance to be edifying to my sisters and brothers, just as your story, your insight, your revelation of God's heart, is something the rest of us need."[33] Rahab had her own redemption story to tell, a one-of-a-kind tale spun through her own unique experiences and follies, strengths and weaknesses, knowledge and insights.

If that overlooked soul you have helped is no ordinary person and has a unique redemption story to tell, then he will not just be the object of your pity; he will be a vessel for experiencing and understanding God's love better. Have we ever considered that we need people like Rahab and Ying for the good of our faith? Maybe our kids need to see people who are different from them so they can practice compassion. Maybe we need to see grace at work in Rahab to remind us what it feels like to be snatched from hopelessness and ushered into the family of God, a memory that may have dimmed in our hearts due to the distractions of life. Maybe new Christians will bring some new passion and new energy to the church family.

The reality is that the overlooked and ignored need us, the church, but we also need them. They need us to notice them. They need our time and our listening ears. They may need some of our physical

---

[33] Andrew Peterson, *Adorning the Dark: Thoughts on Community, Calling, and the Mystery of Making* (Nashville: B&H Publishing Group, 2019), Kindle file, Preface.

blessings. They need us to share the good news with them and pray for them, but *we also need them* to help us renew and grow. It's a new reason for us to reach out with God's love and message—because people need it and so do we!

I currently work in East Asia to help the local church grow. Specifically, I train Christian leaders how to lead and center their personal lives on Christ. I don't often consider that maybe I am there for the good of my own faith. I was reminded of this recently. The local pastors serve faithfully under constant pressure. Most only became Christians as adults. Their work is illegal; the government pressure continues to increase; the pay is not great; their families rarely support it. I'd like to think that I can really help them. But during our hardest year in East Asia, one of these dear brothers said to me, "I know that this season has been really difficult for you. My wife and I pray for you every day." There I was standing outside the coffee shop with him pretending that some of the perpetual dust of our city was caught in my eye, so the brother wouldn't see my tears.

Ying brought more to her church than she will ever realize. Parents, think of the energy it takes to "pew wrestle" two kids in church, even when you are man-to-man, that is, Mom's got one kid and Dad's got the other. My saintly wife was outnumbered by our little monsters three to one while I preached nearly every Sunday, with nothing to defend herself but a diaper bag full of sweet and salty snacks. I picture her backed up against the end of the long, wooden pew, hurling packages of fruit snacks at my kids—"Back! Back, you little terrors." Meanwhile, I was cluelessly preaching about the great blessing of children. That was difficult enough for my wife (or so I hear). Ying showed up for the worship gathering with eight kids by herself—like 300 Spartans versus the entire Persian army. There aren't enough fruit snacks in the world. Yet she still came. This woman continued to participate in the ministry even though she often sat alone at fellowship dinners in Lent. This woman put her kids through parochial school so they could learn about Christ every day. Sure, she probably got some kind of tuition discount, but imagine how much that cost her in money, time, and gas, getting her kids back and forth between a Christian grade school and high school. Learn persistence and faithfulness from this courageous refugee.

It's not surprising that God can encourage us through nobodies like Rahab and Ying. Think of what we have already learned about Jesus when he was brought into this world as our Savior: the unexpected son of a teenage girl. Raised in a poor home in a backwoods town, his followers were mostly outcasts and misfits. He was known as a friend of prostitutes and scumbags. He was nailed naked to a cross along the interstate for everyone to gawk at, for everyone to think, "So this is what happens to losers, the descendant of nobodies like Rahab."

But three days later, he burst out of the tomb, alive. That descendant of a prostitute, a pagan woman, failed kings, liars, thieves, adulterers, and murderers raised you up as the forgiven and loved child of God who will enjoy him forever.

The Nobody Touched by Jesus

I had such a vivid imagination when I was a little boy. Let me offer you a typical example. My mom, who loved to cook, thought it was a good idea for the family to branch out of our Midwestern fare from time to time. She felt we needed to move beyond tater tots and cream of mushroom soup. Pot roast with potatoes and carrots was just too safe, too ordinary, I guess. So one night, she introduced us to something called an avocado. Now, first of all, the name itself raised some red flags for me. Something told me that the Jolly Green Giant wouldn't be caught dead packaging and freezing some vegetable (actually a fruit) called an avocado. And second of all, where did it come from, anyway? Probably some exotic island where they ate sea cucumbers[34] and white, squirmy grubs.

But more than the name, it was the appearance that freaked me out. Now, I want you to imagine a boy, who had been raised on *Star Wars* and *Godzilla,* staring at an avocado that had been halved. Can you see it? The pit is the bone—maybe an elbow. The bright yellow meat is the muscle. Didn't you know that all monsters have flesh the color of mustard? The skin is—well—it's the monster's skin, all bumpy, rough, and green. For the life of me, I could not choke it down. It wasn't until after the age of 40 that I even dreamed of eating it. Even now, it sometimes feels like I'm mushing a bunch of raw meat in my mouth, albeit raw meat with cilantro and lime mixed into it.

Now imagine a boy like that entering an underfunded nursing home in the 1970s to visit his great-grandma. Please remember that I was only probably eight years old at the time before you judge me. In order to get residents out of their rooms for a little interaction and

---

[34] Warning: these are not really cucumbers from the sea, it turns out.

exercise, this small-town Michigan facility would arrange people in their wheelchairs up and down the hallway every afternoon. They looked a little like old paratroopers lined up along each side of their C-47 Skytrains getting ready to jump into battle—though I doubt that any real paratroopers going into a real battle ever fell asleep before the green light came on. Now picture this little kid with an overly active imagination. And picture any zombie movie—ever. Envision him creeping down the middle of that hallway as wrinkly people reached out to shake his hand or touch him. I was HORRIFIED! I was too young to understand that most of them were just lonely and in desperate need of human contact.

We all need human contact to thrive and even survive. The book *Simple Church* tells the story of orphans in countries like Romania and Russia where the ratio of children to adults is dismal. The authors wrote, "A decade ago journalists first entered these orphanages. They were shocked at what they did not see or hear. There was no laughter. No tears. Three-year-olds could not speak or cry."[35] The issue? The lack of attention and nurture and touch. No one ever touched these little ones. No one ever hugged them or even laid a hand gently on their backs to assure them that maybe, just maybe, everything was going to be okay.

Mark 1 tells us how Jesus touched a man that most other people would have avoided at all costs and changed his life forever.

> A man with leprosy came to him and begged him on his knees, "If you are willing, you can make me clean." Filled with compassion, Jesus reached out his hand and touched the man. "I am willing," he said. "Be clean!" Immediately the leprosy left him and he was cured. (Mark 1:40-42 NIV 84)

It's difficult for us to understand the full plight of the leper. This disease is not very common today, but it was fairly common when Jesus walked the earth. There are various kinds of leprosy; the worst

---

[35] Thom S. Rainer and Eric Geiger, *Simple Church* (Nashville: B&H Publishing Group, 2011), p. 154.

kind is called Hansen's disease. Hansen's disease deadens its victims' nerve cells so they can no longer feel pain the way they are supposed to. A leper might step on a nail and walk around with it in his foot for days if he is not careful. Leprosy destroys body tissue so that its victim can lose limbs, eyes, lips, and nose. Imagine how horrible late-stage lepers must look; imagine the terrible odor.

I once ministered to a lady who was dying of gangrene poisoning because she had a blood clot in her hip that doctors couldn't remove. The nurses tried to cover up the stench of decaying flesh with a fan and frightening amounts of vanilla-scented perfume. It didn't work. The room festered with an unbelievable, gagging stench that I will never forget. This would have been the life of many lepers in the days of Jesus.

Furthermore, God's law required lepers to be isolated from the rest of society, in part to control the spread of infection, especially Hansen's disease, for which there was no known cure. Lepers had to wear mourning clothes, leave their hair in disorder, cover their beards, and cry, "Unclean! Unclean!" so that everyone would know to avoid them. As long as the disease lasted, they had to live away from other people (Leviticus 13:45,46). Rabbinic law (not God's law, mind you) demanded that lepers live outside of the city walls, and that was enforced with a severe whipping if they didn't.

Worse yet, rabbis preached that lepers were being punished for committing 1 of 11 sins. So no one was allowed to greet them. If a leper stuck his head through a door, the whole building became unclean. He wasn't allowed within 6 feet of another person. One rabbi boasted how he would even throw stones at the lepers to keep them away.

The compassionate touch of Jesus

In desperation, this leper breaks the 6-foot barrier and falls on his knees at Jesus' feet. Notice Rabbi Jesus' response to this disheveled, malodorous man. Mark says that Jesus was "filled with compassion" for him (1:41 NIV 84). The English word *compassion* comes from a fascinating Greek word used several times in the accounts of Jesus' life. It's the word *splankna,* and it literally means "the guts." *Splankna* sounds to me like noises your stomach might make after eating too much Texas chili. What's the connection between guts and compassion? Greek people believed that your guts were the seat of your emotions. When you are nervous, where do you feel it? In the guts, right? Sometimes, when we are really upset, we even say, "It feels like someone punched me in the gut." So what Mark is literally saying is that when Jesus saw this man, he was nearly sick to his stomach with compassion. It hurt him terribly to see such awful suffering in one of his precious creatures.

In fact, Jesus was so overwhelmed with compassion for this suffering soul that he reached out to touch the leper, to literally *grasp* the man. It is so critical that we do not miss this! When Christian Doctor Paul Brand was working with a leprous man in India, he laid his hand on the man and informed him through a translator about the treatment he would receive. Suddenly, the man began to sob. When Dr. Brand asked if he had said something wrong, the translator responded, "No, Doctor. He says he is crying because you put your hand around his shoulder. Until you came here no one had touched him for many years."

I don't know what was more miraculous to this leprous man—that he was healed or that Jesus touched his rancid, unclean body. Imagine living for years without being touched—no hugs, no handshakes, no pats on the shoulder. Imagine that every time you saw a person—any person, including the people you dearly loved—you had to shout out "Unclean!" and keep away from them. But Jesus touched the man.

We live in a society that is heading further and further down that path of isolation. The deeper we crawl into our secure living room cocoons; the more we surround ourselves with virtual pals through the internet, Facebook, Netflix, and Messenger; the more we live out of our minivans, ordering every meal through a little speaker—the more we distance ourselves from human touch. We still think we're in touch because we're so busy and we're always on our phones, but there is less actual life-on-life contact all the time.

It just seems safer that way, doesn't it? I am editing this book as COVID-19 swings its deadly sickle back and forth across the world. The term *social distancing* was hardly known before 2020; now it is a common household saying. The grocery stores where I live feature bright lines of tape on the floor to show you how far apart you should stand from other shoppers in the checkout line to avoid infection. It's dangerous to get too close.

Many of us by nature would prefer to keep our social distance from certain kinds of people, so we try to minimize contact with them. It's as if we're afraid that if we get closer than six feet from certain kinds of people, we will catch a bad case of the *evils*. As a result, some Christians want the church to be a safe place, in the sense that they don't want to worry about any bad influences on their families in the church. Some Christians send their kids to Christian grade schools, high schools, or colleges not so much for the daily exposure to the Word as for the daily isolation from the leprous touch of the world.

As we wait for Christ to return and restore all things, we are tempted to shut out the evil world and just hang with the people we trust. "The world is going to hell in a handbasket, so good riddance! Let's just stick together and worship and do our own thing until Jesus returns to clean house." And we are tempted to sit in judgment over the world, pointing fingers and complaining about how bad everything and everyone else is. The problem is that evil is not only *out there.* As the famous Pogo comic strip quipped, "We have met the enemy and he is us." The problem with trying to shut out evil is that we take our own evil with us into the fortress. We can't shut out our own sinful nature. It's like running inside a house to get away from an aggressive rattlesnake only to run into the growling pit bull who's been cooped up and starved for a week. When a building, a small group, or a Christian organization becomes our safe place, we have created an idol that will warp our perspective and keep us from God's purposes for our lives.

Social distancing will never keep us safe from the evil world and lost people. Jesus is our only safe place, as the psalmist says: "You are my hiding place; you will protect me from trouble and surround me with songs of deliverance" (Psalm 32:7). It is only the power, love, and acceptance of Jesus that protect us while empowering us to venture into the dark and lonely places of the world, across the street to that family we don't know, to the other side of town where people don't fit into our happy little boxes. As one preacher put it, "The way to avoid sin is not to avoid sinners but to stick close to Jesus."

The church for nobodies is a messy church. Touching lives means that we reach out to people we wouldn't normally be comfortable with—people who have been burned by the church before; people who come with bundles of emotional baggage and may not understand what is socially proper in church groups; people who need a lot of coaching to help them through addictions, brokenness, and past abuse; people who don't always look, dress, talk, or act like we would like or expect; people who voted for the other guy in the last election; people who have some pretty crazy ideas about love and family. But when we touch the lives of others with the name of Christ, we won't get infected with some kind of moral leprosy. In fact, we will find that we are empowered by God's amazing gospel to serve the people we are trying to reach.

The cleansing hand of Jesus

After the compassionate touch of Jesus, we are told that he cured the leper. In fact, the exact words Jesus used were "Be clean!" (Mark 1:41 NIV 84). Jesus cured many diseases, but whenever Jesus cured leprosy, the Bible says that he "cleansed" the leper (Matthew 8:3). Of course, that means that the leprosy itself was eradicated, the nerves and skin restored to normal. It was a miracle, but something else happened too. A man with leprosy was considered ceremonially unclean. He was not allowed to enter the temple; he could never worship with God's people or offer sacrifices. Cleansing meant he could finally return to church and the fellowship of believers. Cleansing also meant that a healed leper could pick up his little girl for the first time in years—maybe she wasn't even so little anymore. He could kiss his wife and snuggle her. He could sit down to dinner with his family, pray with them, and laugh with them again. This cleansing meant that he was transformed into a whole new person with new opportunities. He got his life back.

Showing compassion and touching the lives of others, especially the world's nobodies, takes a lot of time, hard work, and dedication. It's messy; there are setbacks, but to see them slowly cleansed by the grace of God is a marvelous thing.

To be honest, there are people who just don't seem like they are worth our time as we touch their lives with the love and message of Jesus. We might think that they are too far gone, but no one is beyond the reach of God's cleansing love. When Debbie and Lumpy (I don't even remember his given name) asked me to do their wedding, it was the first wedding I had ever performed as a pastor. Lumpy was a character. He owned a junkyard (he called it a "boneyard"), and his business card was something you should not hand out in a mixed crowd. Two of his groomsmen (one was named Jesse James, like the Western outlaw) couldn't attend the wedding because they had both been thrown in jail. Every member of the wedding party showed up at the reception with a bottle of Boone's Farm in each hand.[36] I had to cover my toddler's ears for most of the best man's speech. I didn't think it was a good idea for her to learn all those four-letter words so early in her life. I thought that I just needed to suffer through the whole wedding process and be done with it.

I doubted I would ever see Debbie and Lumpy again. But actually, when I shared the gospel with Lumpy, he was blown away; he had no idea there was a God out there who even loved someone like him so much. He ended up being confirmed as a member at our church. He was the life of the party, and church fellowship gatherings were never the same.

Oh, there were definitely some uncomfortable moments. Like the time Lumpy waved me over at one of our bowling church fellowships. "This is the best **** party I have ever been to," he yelled at one of those ill-timed lulls in conversation so that everyone heard him. It

---

[36] Nothing says classy wedding like double-fistin' Boone's Farm.

was a good party. This *leper* had been cleansed by the gospel and welcomed by God's people.

Look, even if you don't see such immediate and drastic results, touching the lives of others, even in simple ways, is never just wasted sweat. As Maximus says in *Gladiator,* "What we do in life echoes in eternity." Our service in the name of the risen Christ brings blessing and grace to the lives of real people. This world is a better place because of the ways you touch the lives of others. And heaven will be even fuller because people saw Jesus in you and heard about him from you. And there will be even greater joy in heaven because of your service on this earth. Jesus taught his disciples about this:

> "Then the King will say to those on his right, 'Come, you who are blessed by my Father; take your inheritance, the kingdom prepared for you since the creation of the world. For I was hungry and you gave me something to eat, I was thirsty and you gave me something to drink, I was a stranger and you invited me in, I needed clothes and you clothed me, I was sick and you looked after me, I was in prison and you came to visit me.'
> "Then the righteous will answer him, 'Lord, when did we see you hungry and feed you, or thirsty and give you something to drink? When did we see you a stranger and invite you in, or needing clothes and clothe you? When did we see you sick or in prison and go to visit you?'
> "The King will reply, 'Truly I tell you, whatever you did for one of the least of these brothers and sisters of mine, you did for me.'" (Matthew 25:34-40)

From the vantage point of heaven, you will see how all these little ways that you touched the lives of others in the name of Jesus made a difference, bringing cleansing and peace to so many people in ways you never even realized. You will think, "I just gave that homeless guy the other half of my Subway sandwich." "I just let that frazzled mother cut in line." "I just presented that exhausted cashier with a bouquet of flowers." "I just helped my annoying roommate do his homework one night." "I just stopped my car to find out if she was okay." "I just volunteered at the center because I needed something to do." "I just invited him to church on a whim; I never thought he would come." "I just talked to him because he seemed so lonely." And you will have the further joy of knowing that whatever you did for one of the least of these seeming nobodies, you were actually doing for Jesus. You were serving Jesus in that tiny, passing moment. And you were also a physical stand-in for him, serving as his hands and feet and voice—a double blessing that makes an eternal difference.

On May 10, 1873, Father Damien arrived on the island of Molokai, Hawaii, to live and work with the 816 lepers living in the secluded town of Kalaupapa, knowing full well it was probably a death sentence for him. The lepers had been quarantined there by the king of Hawaii to prevent the spread of that horrific disease. After building a church, Father Damien served as priest for years while dressing ulcers and digging graves and building homes, schools, beds, and coffins.

One day, Father Damien accidentally spilled boiling water on his bare foot. He was surprised when he didn't feel anything. So he poured some of the boiling water on his other foot; he didn't feel that either and realized that he had finally contracted leprosy himself.

When beginning his sermons every Sunday morning year after year, he would address the congregation as his "fellow believers." But that following Sunday, he addressed the congregation as his "fellow lepers." In his passion to save them and improve their lives, he eventually became one of them.

In Jesus' passion to save us, he became one of us. It was definitely not safe for him. People not only touched him—some people also laid hands on him, beat him, and nailed him to a cross. But now, he reigns over all the universe in his resurrected body, working through us as his hands and feet and voice to touch the lives of others with his cleansing love.

Part 5

Somebody's Future

Better is one day in your courts than a thousand else-where; I would rather be a doorkeeper in the house of my God than dwell in the tents of the wicked.

—Psalm 84:10

There are only two days on my calendar: this day and that Day.

—Martin Luther

The Chinese Qingming festival, or Tomb-Sweeping Day, is observed every year right around the time of Easter, but the two holidays have very little in common. Qingming revolves around the concept of death, Easter around the concept of life.

Every Qingming festival, Chinese families traditionally visit the tombs of their ancestors to clean up the surrounding area; pray to their ancestors; and make offerings of food, household goods, and joss paper, or "ghost money" (money that the deceased can use in the afterlife).

One of my American friends who lives in China once wished his Chinese friends, "Qingmingjie Kuaile!" or "Happy Tomb-Sweeping Day!" They told him rather firmly that he should never say such a thing. There is nothing happy about tomb-sweeping. Yan Xing writes, "Ancestor worship is being thoughtful of the end and honoring the ancestors; sweeping the graves on Qingming is to show our remembrance of our forefathers. It is on the one hand showing sincere respect, and on the other hand a way of settling with death—deifying ancestors and giving them the ability to watch over descendants, so as to achieve peace and success in reality."[37] There is no real future hope in Qingming.

As we have seen, Jesus' resurrection on Easter guarantees that we will live forever, a joyful escape from the endless ghastly cycle of Qingming. But what will that future look like? What awaits God's somebodies beyond the door of death?

---

[37] https://www.chinasource.org/resource-library/chinese-church-voices/easter-the-way-out-from-qingming/

What Waits for Somebody Special

The sweetest thing in all my life has been the longing—to reach the Mountain, to find the place where all the beauty came from . . . my country, the place where I ought to have been born.

—C. S. Lewis,
Till We Have Faces

"Danny's" father regularly abused him, his three sisters, and his mom. Though Dad made decent money at a local steel mill, the family never saw it. He spent so much on drugs that there wasn't enough to buy decent food for the home. Danny's mom frequently resorted to baking Crisco and flour biscuits for meals; Danny vividly recalls the crippling burn of acid reflux as a preschooler.

Occasionally, Danny's mom would pack up the kids and leave his father, but they always went back.

Around 1980, they finally left Dad for good. They fled to the Salvation Army, and from there they migrated to the East Coast, where they lived on the streets. Danny's mom regularly wandered off to party, abandoning Danny and his sister (ages 6 and 5 at the time) to fend for themselves. At night, they slept on the steps of a church, beneath bridges, or under the piers at the beach.

One day during this traumatic season, Danny's mom gave the kids a package of Oreos. Seeing an opportunity to improve their lot, Danny made a business proposal to his sister: "We'll eat some and sell the rest." So these two homeless grade-schoolers wandered the strand, hawking cookies for 10 cents apiece to sunbaked tourists. Then they invested their meager profits in a new package of Oreos. They ate some of those, sold the rest, and so on.

For a while, Danny and his sister holed up in an abandoned house littered with people doing drugs and sleeping wherever. After discovering a mess of discarded mini golf passes, they practiced their putt when they weren't running their Oreo business. It was something to pass the time.

Danny recalls that they didn't really celebrate Christmas during that time; in fact, one year, the only present he received was a Happy Meal toy.

By God's grace, a friend eventually reported their dreadful situation to the local authorities. The kids were put into the foster system, and this friend's parents attained custody of them. It was the best home life Danny ever experienced during his childhood. When the kids arrived home from school, there were snacks on the table, like they saw on TV and always imagined family life would be like. Their foster parents would help them with their homework; they had their own bedrooms; Christmas, Halloween, birthdays—all the holidays that kids love and are supposed to enjoy—were amazing!

They only stayed at this house of healing for a year, but as a 38-year-old man, Danny would still speak of that season of life with tremulous emotion, deeply grateful for foster parents who showed him what a real home was.

Sehnsucht—going home

Home. It's a word drenched with emotion. For some of us, that simple word basks in a glow of fond, peaceful memories—wrapped up in a blanket by a warm fire or gathered around a dazzling Christmas tree late at night with your favorite people. For some of us, that four-letter word flattens us with a flood of toxicity, of pain and fear, shame and regret. For the rest of us, *home* is a mix of memories, both positive and negative. Regardless of your experiences and feelings about it, however, that simple word *home* seems to generate a deep emotional, almost painful, longing in the soul.

Where does that longing come from? German philosophers call it *Sehnsucht,* a word that has no accurate translation into English. You might render it as "longing" or "intensely missing," but that doesn't quite catch the flavor. Wikipedia says, "It is this close relationship (encapsulated in one word) between ardent longing or yearning *(das Sehnen)* and addiction *(die Sucht)* that lurks behind each longing." C. S. Lewis described it as the "inconsolable longing" in the human heart for "we know not what." Psychology Wiki further defines it this way: "It is sometimes felt as a longing for a far-off country, but not a particular earthly land which we can identify. Furthermore there is something in the experience which suggests this far-off country is very familiar and indicative of what we might otherwise call 'home.'" Look for it, and you will quickly discover this *Sehnsucht* in countless poems and songs of every generation and genre. There's "Home" by Michael Bublé and a completely different song called "Home" by Daughtry; "Sweet Home Alabama" by Lynyrd Skynyrd; "Take Me Home, Country Roads" by John Denver; "Home Sweet Home" by Mötley Crüe; "I'll Be Home for Christmas" by Bing Crosby. The list is nearly endless.

Everyone has feelings of *Sehnsucht* to a certain extent at different times in their lives—and not just when they are old. I remember being physically stricken with it as a grade-schooler while reading the closing chapter of *The Lord of the Rings,* when Frodo sails west from the Grey Havens. It's an inconsolable longing for something that nothing in this world can fully satisfy. Many of us have felt this deeply when reminiscing about our childhood home.

Maybe you have had this strange experience: You had the opportunity to return to the place you grew up. You rediscovered all your old haunts. You once again strolled the lanes where you played street hockey and rode your bike; you pointed out the barbershop where you got all your haircuts and the lake where you liked to fish for bluegill. But it wasn't home anymore. Old neighbors had painted their siding a different color; the Korean family moved out; the drugstore closed; they put a stoplight in along Main Street. So much has changed. Besides that, you've changed. You aren't the same fourth grader that you were, riding your banana seat bike with your mop of thick hair.[38] It's not really home anymore.

It doesn't just happen with home. Think of the buildup to the holidays. It rarely meets our lofty expectations. The turkey and the stuffing, the pumpkin pie and presents, the holly and the ivy . . . the inevitable public meltdown between your dad and his sister, the uncle who is already slurring his words before you sit down to dinner, the frantic rush to find gifts for your nieces and nephews because you found out that your sister bought all your kids presents this year, the awkward office parties. Even the lovely parts rush by so quickly. Or we play that video game all the way until we have obliterated the final boss. Now what? Or we save up and buy that car we always wanted, and we sit in it wondering if we should have. We push ourselves to be the best; we reach the top; we look down and we wonder, "Is this all there is?" Actually, it's all *Sehnsucht*—trying to get home or back home.

Where does that inconsolable longing come from? Our first parents, Adam and Eve, were truly home in the Garden of Eden with God. They walked with him in perfect fellowship, harmony, and joy. But when they rebelled, they were kicked out of that garden, and the way back in was shut forever by an angelic warrior with a flaming sword. Ever since then, we have all been on an eternal quest to get back to the garden—only it no longer exists this side of heaven, and sinful people would not be allowed back in if it did. This is finally the foundational issue behind all of the feelings of nobody-ness and the desperate pursuits of somebody-ness. C. S. Lewis wrote, "These things—the beauty, the memory of our own past—are good images of what we really desire; but if they are mistaken for the thing itself they turn into dumb idols, breaking the hearts of their worshipers. For they are not the thing itself." We're not home, and we know it.

Even those who follow Christ have this inconsolable longing. We hear it in the apostle Paul's words in 2 Corinthians 5:1,2, "We know

---

[38] What ever happened to banana seats? I felt they were much more comfortable and safer and easier for sharing rides.

that if the earthly tent we live in is destroyed, we have a building from God, an eternal house in heaven, not built by human hands. Meanwhile we groan, longing to be clothed instead with our heavenly dwelling." It is a longing for our true home, our eternal home, where we will finally come face-to-face with our Savior.

Our heavenly dwelling

> All their life in this world and all their adventures had only been the cover and the title page: now at last they were beginning Chapter One of the Great Story which no one on earth has read: which goes on for ever: in which every chapter is better than the one before.

—C. S. Lewis, The Last Battle

God originally created *this* world to be our eternal home, and everything worked exactly the way it was designed to work. But since Adam and Eve were driven from that home, the world has been in a perpetual state of spiritual and physical decay. We are continually surrounded by evil, pain, and death. The news is nothing but a litany of depravity and destruction. Even after all our advances in medicine, babies are still born with horrible deformities, and perfectly healthy people waste away in horrific diseases. Pandemics ravage whole countries—even the world. Evil people continually hurt helpless victims, and families are shattered with selfishness. Governments rise and fall; oppression is everywhere. Everything breaks down, falls apart, rusts away. We struggle with so much pain, setback, sorrow, and sin—our sin and the sin of others—and we cannot escape it. We cannot bar the doors of our homes or our churches and wish it away. It seeps in through the windows and the cracks in the floor; in fact, it lurks within us, at least in our sinful natures and broken bodies. I think we can all agree that Humpty Dumpty has been smashed to pieces—the world is falling apart—and there is no way all the king's horses and all the king's men are going to put Humpty back together again. Scientists, philosophers, and politicians have been trying for centuries; we're not making any headway. Sure, technology is advancing exponentially, but we humans are stuck.

When Jesus came to this earth, he performed many miracles to testify to his deity, strengthen the faith of his followers, and offer us a glimpse of the way that things *were supposed to be*. The miracles offered people a glorious snapshot of Home (capital *H*), but they were not Home itself. We might call them a temporary, simple reversal of the effects of sin. For example, when Jesus raised his friend Lazarus from the dead, it was a *simple reversal*. Jesus called Lazarus back to this world in his old body, a body that was still subject to sin, sickness, pain, and death. In fact, Lazarus eventually got sick and died again. And so, on this earth, we have found ways to slow down the process of decay and stave off death for a bit, even to enjoy the fruits of our labors from time to time. But it doesn't last; it cannot last; hence, the foolishness of pursuing somebody-ness in this world.

Jesus' resurrection, however, is what C. S. Lewis called "the Great Reversal." In other words, Jesus rose in glory with a glorified body no longer affected by sin, sickness, pain, and death. He is the guarantee that someday things will go back to the way they were supposed to be, the way they were at Home, in the Garden of Eden. The day is coming soon (really soon, I hope) when the resurrected Jesus will return in power to restore all things, to give us back the Home we lost and have longed for our entire lives. The apostle Paul tells us that on that day, all of creation will finally be liberated from its bondage to decay (Romans 8:21).

In the book of Revelation, the apostle John paints stunning pictures of this Home you can confidently anticipate through Jesus' Great Reversal:

> Then one of the elders asked me, "These in white robes—
> who are they, and where did they come from?"
>
> I answered, "Sir, you know."
>
> And he said, "These are they who have come out of the great tribulation; they have washed their robes and made them white in the blood of the Lamb. Therefore,

they are before the throne of God and serve him day and night in his temple; and he who sits on the throne will shelter them with his presence. 'Never again will they hunger; never again will they thirst. The sun will not beat down on them,' nor any scorching heat. For the Lamb at the center of the throne will be their shepherd; 'he will lead them to springs of living water.' 'And God will wipe away every tear from their eyes.'" (Revelation 7:13-17)

Then I saw "a new heaven and a new earth," for the first heaven and the first earth had passed away, and there was no longer any sea. I saw the Holy City, the new Jerusalem, coming down out of heaven from God, prepared as a bride beautifully dressed for her husband. And I heard a loud voice from the throne saying, "Look! God's dwelling place is now among the people, and he will dwell with them. They will be his people, and God himself will be with them and be their God. 'He will wipe every tear from their eyes. There will be no more death' or mourning or crying or pain, for the old order of things has passed away." (Revelation 21:1-4)

Then the angel showed me the river of the water of life, as clear as crystal, flowing from the throne of God and of the Lamb down the middle of the great street of the city. On each side of the river stood the tree of life, bearing twelve crops of fruit, yielding its fruit every month. And the leaves of the tree are for the healing of the nations. No longer will there be any curse. The throne of God and of the Lamb will be in the city, and his servants will serve him. They will see his face, and his name will be on their foreheads. There will be no more night. They will not need the light of a lamp or the light of the sun, for the Lord God will give them light. And they will reign for ever and ever. (Revelation 22:1-5)

After a particularly good sermon about heaven, one parishioner told his pastor, "You just made me want to die and go to heaven." The pastor wasn't quite sure if it was meant to be a compliment or a jab. But honestly, after you read John's words, don't you long even more for your heavenly home? Even on our best days, when we feel like the king of the world, it is nothing like what John is picturing here.

"The old order of things has passed away." First of all, stated negatively, there will be no more floods, hurricanes, or famines. No more evil people exploiting the helpless; no more war, terrorism, destruction, robbery, or abuse—of any kind. No more aches, pains, or diseases. No more crippling arthritis; no more migraines. No more getting old and dying. No more orphanages or palliative care. No more cancer centers, braille, wheelchairs, or hospital beds. No more homeless kids selling Oreos at the beach and sleeping in crack houses. I'm sick of the news. I'm sick of people getting blown up and mutilated. I'm sick of hearing about helpless people starving to death when there is more than enough food for the entire world or living on $1.50 a day and dying of diarrhea because their water is putrid. I'm sick of hearing about human trafficking and how the pornography industry destroys the lives of countless girls, girls with souls and daddies who couldn't or wouldn't protect them. No more. Jesus will obliterate all that is evil and wrong while preserving us, his priceless somebodies.

In a positive way, the lame will line dance, the blind will see brilliant color, and the deaf will hear enchanting sonatas for the very first time. Every ache and pain will be obliterated once and for all. Jesus personally will wipe away every last tear from our eyes; the heartbreaking memories from this life, if we still even have them, will be redeemed in the comfort of our Savior's almighty power and boundless love. We won't ever again wrestle with fears, feelings of shame, or the plague of nobody-ness. Death will be a distant memory. It will be like stepping permanently from a frigid snowy porch into the warmth and comfort of our living room—to forget about the wind and winter forever.

And how we will be changed! The apostle Paul writes, "So will it be with the resurrection of the dead. The body that is sown is perishable, it is raised imperishable; it is sown in dishonor, it is raised in glory; it is sown in weakness, it is raised in power; it is sown a natural body, it is raised a spiritual body" (1 Corinthians 15:42-44). If you're stumbling over the perishable/imperishable thing, just think about perishable food, like fresh bananas. What happens when you leave those bananas out a little too long? They break down into brown and gushy bags of goo. Our bodies are perishable; they are breaking down. If you are still around in 25 years, you won't be the same svelte, handsome rock star that you are now—more like a bag of goo and a little less like a rock star, anyway. But when we arrive Home, Jesus, "by the power that enables him to bring everything under his control, will transform our lowly bodies so that they will be like his glorious body" (Philippians 3:21). I am not even quite sure what that means. I don't know that it means you will look like Mr. or Mrs. Universe, but your body will be perfect.

And then the wedding supper of the Lamb will commence, with Christ and all of his people of all time gathered together at the table, all of those nobodies who became somebodies by his grace: "a feast of rich food for all peoples, a banquet of aged wine—the best of meats and the finest of wines" (Isaiah 25:6). Imagine the laughter and the stories. If it helps you, picture the Great Hall of Hogwarts during the school's opening feast; the Cratchit home where Bob is slicing into a turkey twice the size of Tiny Tim, a turkey sent by the reformed Mr. Scrooge; four weary hobbits feasting for hours in the home of Tom Bombadil and Goldberry, his stunning bride; the woodland animals toasting one another with refreshing strawberry cordial in Redwall Abbey. Choose your picture; they all invoke the *Sehnsucht* that will finally be fulfilled at this table, merely hors d'oeuvres that awkwardly anticipate the glorious reality.

And then we will serve our God forever and ever. I remember one student telling me he wasn't all that interested in heaven because he didn't really like to sing. That's a pretty stunted view of heaven. When we arrive Home, we will commence our different heavenly vocations. We will not just be singing and playing harps but work-ing our Home—the new heaven and earth—for the glory of God like we were always intended to do. Other people think, *When I get to heaven, I don't want to work. I want to rest.* They picture heaven as this health spa where they will lounge around for eternity. I get it; work here often stinks because of Adam's curse. But imagine being able to finally do what we were always supposed to do and be what we were always supposed to be, forever, without the frustrations and setbacks of this broken world. Then can truly say, at the end of every day, "It was a good day at work."

After years of wandering, we will finally be Home, and life will truly begin. Martin Luther said, "[God] wants us to become sure that our present life is not yet our destiny, but that we are to expect another life, which is to be our true life. Just as the sun is waiting for a new attire to be given it, and the earth and all other creatures; a cleansing from the misuse by the devil and the world."

I once ministered to a dying Christian lady in the hospital who kept telling her family that she wanted to go home. They would always respond, "Mom, you can't go home; you're too sick." When she kept insisting, it dawned on me that maybe she was not talking about her house. I shared this with her family, and the next time she said it, they told her, "Go home, Mom. It's okay." She seemed more at peace. Shortly after that, she died and went Home. Dearest child of God, that's where you belong! That's Home in the truest sense.

A lot of Christian music focuses on how God will help us through our earthly struggles. That's great, because we often need to be reminded that God is our ever-present help in time of need. But there is so much more than this life we are struggling through. One precious treasure the old hymn writers gave us was their eternal perspective. They elevate our eyes to what is beyond this world, as Paul said in Colossians, "Since, then, you have been raised with Christ, set your hearts on things above, where Christ is, seated at the right hand of God" (3:1). After all, that is our true Home.

> *Jerusalem the golden, With milk and honey blest—*
> *The sight of it refreshes The weary and oppressed:*

I know not, oh, I know not What joys await us there,
What radiancy of glory, What bliss beyond compare.

—Bernard of Cluny, tr. John Mason Neale,
"Jerusalem the Golden"

A few years ago, a dying 14-year-old girl wanted to be cryogenically frozen. Her case was taken to court, and this was her letter to the judge: "I have been asked to explain why I want this unusual thing done. I'm only 14 years old and I don't want to die, but I know I am going to. I think being cryo-preserved gives me a chance to be cured and woken up, even in hundreds of years' time. I don't want to be buried underground. I want to live and live longer and I think that in the future they may find a cure for my cancer and wake me up. I want to have this chance. This is my wish." There is no way I could ever understand her plight. I have never been through something so horrible, but I do want to tell her that, even if this doesn't work out for her, Jesus offers her more than just a simple reversal that will give her a few extra years on this broken planet. He offers her the Great Reversal where cancer will be history. He offers to take her Home.

There is no joy like the joy of heaven,
for in that state are no sad divisions,
unchristian quarrels,
contentions, evil designs,
weariness, hunger, cold,
sadness, sin, suffering,
persecutions, toils of duty.
O healthful place where none are sick!
O happy land where all are kings!
O holy assembly where all are priests!
How free a state where none are servants
except to thee!
Bring me speedily to the land of joy.

—From the Puritan Prayer "Joy"

The Ultimate Somebody

The Lord himself will come down from heaven, with a loud command, with the voice of the archangel and with the trumpet call of God, and the dead in Christ will rise first. After that, we who are still alive and are left will be caught up together with them in the clouds to meet the Lord in the air. And so we will be with the Lord forever. Therefore encourage one another with these words.

—1 Thessalonians 4:16-18

For many of us growing up, our father was the center of our world. His smile made us smile. His frown made us cry. This is perfectly illustrated by a particular photograph of my father and me when I was a four-year-old. Dad and I are sitting together on the couch. His legs are stretched out and his feet are resting on the coffee table. I am desperately trying to stretch myself out in the same way and rest my feet on the same table. The problem is that I am not long enough. So I look like a rickety bridge spanning a yawning chasm, ready to collapse. I imagine I was horribly uncomfortable, but I didn't care; I wanted to be just like him. My dad was the center of my world at that time.

In Revelation 5:5,6, we are given this picture of heaven: "'See, the Lion of the tribe of Judah, the Root of David, has triumphed. He is able to open the scroll and its seven seals.' Then I saw a Lamb, looking as if it had been slain, standing at the center of the throne." In these words, Jesus is called "the Lion of Judah" and the "Lamb" who is standing at the center of the throne. That's an interesting phrase: "the center of the throne." Have you ever been to a throne room? In a throne room, everything is focused on the throne. It is usually ornate, made of gold, and raised up on a platform. All the royal attendants face it at all times, unwilling to turn their backs on the king. In other words, it is the center of the room. Now, our lesson says that the Lamb, Jesus, is "standing at the *center* of the throne." The throne is already at the center of heaven, and Jesus is at the center of that throne. Here's the point: Jesus is the center of the center. Colossians 1:15-17 explains it this way: "The Son is the image of the invisible God, the firstborn over all creation. For in him all things were created: things in heaven and on earth, visible and invisible, whether thrones or powers or rulers or authorities; all things have been created through him and for him. He is before all things, and in him all things hold together." The whole universe bends in on the gravity of Jesus. He is the Center of the center, the Greatest Somebody.

That helps us get a better idea, one final time in this book, what sin really is and why it is such a big deal to God. When we think of sin, we generally think of murder, stealing, or adultery—doing bad things—but sin is putting anything or anyone into the center of our world in the place of Jesus, even good things. When we put our reputation in the center of our lives in a desperate attempt to become somebody and seek value from family, friends, and coworkers instead of Jesus, it's going against the spiritual gravity of the entire universe—it's trying to replace the Center of the center with me. Preaching sermons is a good thing, but when I do it so people will tell me how well I did or what a godly person I am, I have just shoved Jesus off the throne and put myself there. A feeling of security is a good thing, but when we put it in the center of our lives and work excessive hours to the neglect of our family, we are replacing the Center with ourselves. Whenever you put your identity, your success or security, or your own hopes and dreams at the center of your world, you are working against the spiritual gravity of the universe, where Christ is the Center of the center, and it will only end in frustration.

The greatest aspect of heaven won't be the food, as if we are on some divine dinner cruise. It won't be all the grand music. It won't be the lack of sickness, mourning, pain, and death. It won't even be seeing all of our Christian loved ones who arrived before us. It will be Christ, the Center of the center.

Maybe you have a T-shirt signed by LeBron James or a photo of you with some famous somebody. Maybe you shook the president's hand once or competed on *The Price Is Right.* For me, I once sang "Rock and Roll" by Led Zeppelin with Danny Bonaduce's studio band in some cramped Chicago bar. You know who Danny Bonaduce is, right? You don't? Come on! He was the bassist on that old '70s TV show called *The Partridge Family,* featuring David Cassidy. Anyone? Anyway, the crowd went wild. They wanted more, but the lead guitarist said angrily, "We're going to play our own songs now!" That was my 15 minutes of fame.

But that is absolutely nothing—NOTHING—in the universe where Christ sits at the center of the center. Earth is not about me! Heaven is not about me! The universe, present and future, is not about me! It's all about Jesus. Everything! Every word of Scripture (John 5:39), every moment of history, every minute atom is about him. If we cannot get that through our thick skulls, heaven will not be our home.

The Lion and the Lamb who was slain

That's a little scary, but let me close with a few reminders who exactly stands at the center of the center. Remember, Jesus is the Lamb who was "slain." The Center of the center was crushed, destroyed, murdered. The Center of the center humbly let himself become the lowest of the low, a nobody. He allowed himself to experience the disappointment, pain, and hell of what happens to people who foolishly put decaying things at the center of their lives. He was crushed under the weight of our silly expectations and misplaced priorities. He did that so you could be released from your shame forever, so you could know that you really do have value—not in your accomplishments but in the accomplishments of Jesus. Not in the number of likes on your Facebook page but in the joy of knowing that the Center of the center cares about you. Even in heaven we will see the scars of Jesus as a constant reminder of how he became a nobody so we could be saved.

I have visited the famous Terracotta Army of Xi'an, China, on three separate occasions. The setting at the foot of the mountains is breathtaking. The warriors are intricately and uniquely fashioned—no two are alike. You can see hundreds of them lined up, ready for battle. It's estimated that there are more than 8,000 soldiers, 130 chariots with 520 horses, and 150 cavalry horses, most of them still waiting to be unearthed and reassembled. But what most people don't know is that all these warriors are just a small fraction of Emperor Qin Shi Huang's tomb. Other pits in the monstrous expanse hold terracotta officials, acrobats, musicians, and animals. All of this for a man who thought he was so much of a somebody that he made everybody serve him; the project involved 700,000 workers.[39] And all of this not to bless the people in some way but to prepare for the death of their emperor. How different than Jesus. Thousands of people gave their lives in service to this mortal emperor. But we believe that one man, Jesus, was slain so that countless people could be somebodies with him forever.

Meditate also for a moment on those two names given to Jesus in Revelation 5. First, Jesus is called a Lion. The Field Museum in Chicago has preserved two famous Tsavo lions. They give you goosebumps just to look at them, even stuffed and harmless. In March of 1898, the British started building a railway bridge over the Tsavo River in Kenya. During the next nine months of construction, those two lions (now stuffed in Chicago) stalked the campsite, dragging Indian workers from their tents at night and devouring them. Crews tried to scare off the lions with campfires; they built thorn fences around the camp, but the lions just crawled through them. Hundreds of workers eventually fled. No sane person has ever had a pet lion. Nobody teases a lion unless it is behind 4 inches of glass at a zoo. Even then, it is scary to watch it pace and terrifying if it stares you

---

[39] *Slaves* would probably be a more accurate term.

in the eye. You are just a walking meal to that lion. Jesus is the Lion of Judah. He is the risen, ascended, almighty Lord of the universe. Don't tease him; don't play games with him! Psalm 2:12 says, "Kiss the Son, lest he be angry, and you perish in the way, for his wrath is quickly kindled" (ESV).

But Jesus is also a Lamb. In fact, Jesus is called a Lamb 30 times in the book of Revelation. When you think of a lamb, what's your first impression? Fluffy, gentle, harmless. No one ever chose *lambs* for the name of their sports team. "Today's lineup: the Detroit Lions and your very own Las Vegas Lambs!" To make the picture even stranger, this humble lamb looks as if he has been slain—extremely vulnerable, humble, and gentle. It reminds me of what Isaiah prophesied about Jesus, "He will not shout or cry out, or raise his voice in the streets. A bruised reed he will not break, and a smoldering wick he will not snuff out" (Isaiah 42:2,3).

What's the point? If Jesus were all power and no love, gentleness, or humility, he might just devour you in anger or even selfishness. All power and no love lead to oppression. On the other hand, if he were all love, gentleness, or humility but no power, he doesn't have any more control over our lives or future than we do. He might be really encouraging, but encouragement alone is no help if your life is about to fall apart, if danger and trouble come. But your Savior is the Lion and the Lamb, a perfect combination of power and love, the only kind of person you would want holding your future.

This is so helpful for us in our somebody-nobody struggles right now. Sometimes we struggle in our faith walk because we forget that Jesus is a Lion. We make our own plans and expect him to follow us. Sometimes we treat him like a good luck charm, as a way to achieve our somebody dreams, and sometimes we leave him behind for those dreams. However, wise people do not tease a lion or ignore it. Other times we struggle in our faith walk because we forget that Jesus is a Lamb. Whenever trouble comes, or even threatens us, we often cave in to fear because we don't believe he really loves us or has our best interests in mind. We feel we need to take care of ourselves if we are going to survive. But Jesus is for you—who can stand against you?

The result is that you can be as gentle as a lamb when life doesn't follow your plan. You don't need to blow up, scream, or curse your enemies. The Lion is still in charge. It will all turn out, no matter how much people mistreat or malign you, no matter how you have failed or let someone down. You can also be as courageous as a lion when facing total uncertainty, new challenges, the rejection of others, or being a nobody in the eyes of the world. You can roar without fear when Jesus takes you down a path you never would have chosen. It's bound to be filled with danger or adventure, but he is with you every step of the way.

Everything will be okay because Christ is the Center of the center.

Step by step, day by day, year by year, he will guide you until he takes you Home. And when he does, everything else—all your worries, concerns, struggles, shame, pain, hurts—will dissipate like the billowing mists of a crisp mountain morning. Sometimes it feels like the struggle between feeling like a nobody and fighting to become somebody will plague us forever. But your God promises you that someday, when you see Jesus face-to-face, everything will fall into place. You will understand with perfect clarity who you are and whose you are and who Jesus is and how you both fit together. You will think to yourself, *This is what it was all about. This is what I longed for my entire life, to stand before HIM—the one who died and rose to make me somebody special. The Lion/Lamb who powerfully and lovingly walks with me through every earthly struggle. The Center of the center who will take care of me forever, not from some high-powered office in his holy high-rise but from right here, face-to-face—the Greatest Somebody, together with me for eternity.*

> *O highest joy by mortals won,*
> *True Son of God and Mary's Son,*
> *The highborn King of ages!*
> *In your blest body let me be,*

E'en as the branch is in the tree,
Your life my life supplying.
Sighing, Crying
For the savor
Of your favor,
Resting never
Till I rest in you forever.

—Philipp Nicolai,
"How Lovely Shines the Morning Star"

Epilogue

Remember Dale, the nobody I mentioned in the prologue, the raging hater who would meet me for breakfast so he could curse and vent? There in that greasy spoon over those greasy eggs, Christ began to work redemption in his heart, as he repeatedly confessed his depravity to me.

I told him how God has a habit of starting over with the most unlikely characters and how God was doing the same with him. We talked about Noah. I assured him that God did not choose Noah because he was such a righteous person, as many children's Bibles would have you believe (Noah good; other people bad). In fact, the account of Noah contains the Bible's first use of the word *grace,* or "undeserved love." "Noah found favor [grace] in the eyes of the Lord" (Genesis 6:8). Noah was a nobody by nature, just like everybody else, but God had to start over somewhere, and Noah was his choice. The following verse tells us that Noah was a righteous man[40] but only after he experienced God's grace. God had started over with Noah, and now God was starting over with Dale, who had a daughter on the way and was trying to become a dad to his girlfriend's two kids.

From that time on, he earnestly endeavored to capitalize on the restart God had granted him. He still made many mistakes, but he kept returning to Christ's unchanging grace for the strength to try again. Christine and I even invited Dale, his girlfriend, and their kids over to our house a few times. A few years before, I wouldn't let my wife and daughter near him, and now he was in our home!

---

[40] Literally, "complete," not "blameless" or "sinless." He was just like everyone else. Professor John Jeske writes, "There was . . . a completeness, an all-around quality to Noah's faith. Living, as he did, in an ungodly world, his faith was not confined to his heart, but showed itself also in his life, which was devoted to God" (Wisconsin Lutheran Seminary digital essay file).

I would encourage him and pray with him occasionally, even after I moved to another state. He was preparing to become a godly husband. He got a job, bought a trailer, and worked nights. He was trying to become a good father too. He spent more time with the kids and even tried reading the Bible to them. He was still too harsh when disciplining them, but he was working on it. He personally read the Bible, prayed, went to a counselor, and joined a men's small group at a local church.

One day, Dale left me a voicemail that illustrated just how much he had changed. His girlfriend had broken up with him, and he wanted me to hear the draft of a letter he was writing to show her where he was in life now. He said, "The Lord has been with me so far, and he will go with me into the future. You and I had some great, fun times together. You were my first real, true love. . . . I will pray for you and trust God will guide me in the years ahead." I'm not sure she ever received the letter.

Two weeks later, he was gone. Someone had shot him multiple times in the chest and left him for dead in his mobile home. It was days before anyone found his body.

He was a nobody, and not many people mourned his death. The police did some initial investigation into his murder, but they quickly dismissed the case, claiming there were no solid leads. He was a scoundrel, and that's what happened to guys like him.

A few years later a new investigator reopened the case, and the father of Dale's girlfriend was eventually convicted of the murder. Such a dramatic trial made the papers, of course, but Dale was still a nobody, and folks quickly forgot the whole matter.

I still vividly recall an astonishing interview with Dale's brother on a local TV station shortly after his death. "Dale was a deeply spiritual man," he said. Dale? The nobody who hated God and everyone else? The useless drug user who had murdered people before being murdered himself?

Yep, that Dale.

He had become God's somebody, and it transformed his life forever. Now he reigns with Christ.